Meanwhile, I Keep Dancing

CHRISTIE GOODMAN

Auctus Publishers

AuctusPublishers.com

Published by Auctus Publishers
606 Merion Avenue, First Floor
Havertown, PA 19083
Printed in the United States of America

ISBN (Print): 979-8-9915910-0-3
ISBN (Electronic): 979-8-9915910-1-0
Library of Congress Control Number: 2024946718

To my husband, Dave, who holds me up in all situations, and my mother, who did the holding up before him (and sometimes still).

My life in a poem
★ ★ ★

I GET UP.

I WALK.

I FALL DOWN.

MEANWHILE, I KEEP DANCING.

(DANIELLE HILLEL)

Contents

Section One

When Life Falls Apart.

45 years old...

Sometimes healing looks like falling apart.
(Jeanette LeBlanc)

CHAPTER 1

The Night That Changed It All

As I pushed my cart towards the parking lot, the automatic doors opened into the pouring rain. A man wearing a uniform and a Walmart name tag stepped between my cart and the doorway. He was flanked by two other men and a woman who looked like she had just been pulled off her work at a cash register. "Ma'am," he said, "You need to step in here," and he indicated an office off to the side.

I stared at him, confused. "Ma'am," he said again, "We believe there are things in your cart which you haven't paid for. We need you to step into this room so we can take a look."

Haven't paid for? In my cart?

He pointed towards an open door to my left, put his hand on my cart and moved us all back out of the rain. The doors slid shut behind us. I turned towards the door he had indicated, my knuckles gripping tightly to the handle of my cart. The room was small. My cart wouldn't fit inside. I stopped, again confused.

"Ma'am," he said. "You need to go inside while we tally up what is in your cart. Give me the receipt. Just leave the cart with me."

I pried my hands off the handle. In one hand, I had been gripping a roll of birthday wrapping paper with pictures of cakes and candles on it. I stared at it for a moment, then handed it over to him. He handed it off to his team as he led me into a small office and sat me on a bench. The woman slipped into the corner and the other men scattered.

What was going on here? There was something I needed. There was something I needed now.

"Sir," I said, "my blood sugar. It's low and I think I'm in danger of passing out. I need orange juice or something." He must have gone and gotten it because the next thing I remember, I was holding a bottle of orange juice. I fumbled with my purse, pulling out a handful of quarters and dimes. I held them towards him, and he brushed my hand away. "It's fine." He said. "Just forget it."

I unscrewed the cap on the orange juice and swallowed the whole bottle down. I sat, breathing heavily, as he and his team finished tallying up my cart. I looked around in confusion. Now, what was going on again?

The man came in and sat behind a desk. "Ma'am," he said, "Half of the contents of your cart is not on this receipt. You were shoplifting. Do you want to tell me why, or should we just call the police?"

***

When I was first diagnosed with Chronic Fatigue Syndrome, most doctors still thought it didn't exist. They called it the "yuppie flu" and gave me advice like, "Just make yourself do normal things and you will be fine," "Get a hobby," or "Move out of your mother's house and get a life." But I had more hobbies, more interests, than anyone else I knew. And I lived with my mother only because I was too weak to walk across a room by myself. Nationwide, so many doctors believed this illness wasn't real that when congress voted to give five million dollars to the Center for Disease Control to study it, the CDC gave that money to other departments rather than "wasting it" on an illness that didn't exist. If one of my doctors prescribed anything to "help" me, it was depression pills. And to be fair, over the years as I got sicker and sicker and doctors continually told me it was just laziness, I *was* sometimes depressed. But I knew, *knew* that the depression was the result, not the cause of my problems.

When I did find a doctor who believed I was sick and that Chronic Fatigue Syndrome really existed, there still wasn't a lot they could do for me. Few doctors knew much about Chronic Fatigue Syndrome. Any treatment options we came up with resulted from my own ideas as I taught my doctors what I knew from my own experiences and whatever meager research I could find. None of the treatments we did try helped.

That didn't mean I wasn't grateful when finally, after years of searching for someone who would believe in me, I found a doctor who started from the assumption that I was telling the truth. I wasn't lazy; I had plenty of hobbies. Something was physically wrong. He ran all the tests; he asked all the questions. Finally, he gave me a diagnosis: Chronic Fatigue Syndrome. I cried. He shuffled uncomfortably and handed me a tissue. "You aren't going to find a lot of easy answers. Most of my colleagues still think this disease doesn't exist. But it does. We may not understand it, but what you have is real."

I held this diagnosis to my chest like a life preserver. I took it with me everywhere I went. It didn't matter if the next doctor didn't agree. I had a diagnosis, and I clung to it.

But that first doctor was right. There weren't any easy answers. There weren't any answers at all, actually. Aside from the moral support (which, make no mistake, meant the world to me) I was still on my own.

***

I sat in the security office of my local Walmart, rain pouring down outside, and tried to make sense of what was happening. The orange juice had cleared my head a little and adrenalin was staving off the collapse which, just moments before, I had been sure would come. But I still couldn't figure out what was going on.

The head of security finished tallying up my cart and came into the room, closing the door behind him. He showed me my receipt. Then he put another

4

piece of paper next to it. That paper was a handwritten list which I couldn't make sense of. They were simple words. But I couldn't read a sing lone.

He pointed to the handwritten list. "This is everything you had in your cart that is not on the receipt. It's all stolen. You stole all this stuff. You need to tell me why." I looked at the receipt. I looked at the list beside it. The letters swam in front of my eyes. But the meaning was clear. I had stolen it all.

"Why?" He asked me, "Why did you do it?"

I didn't know. I *wanted* to answer him. I just didn't *know* why.

"Ma'am. You have to tell me why you did this. Then I can decide if I am going to call the police. Why did you steal, Ma'am? Why did you do it?"

I didn't know. I tried to come up with an answer. Why was I stealing? Was I just a basically dishonest person? I didn't think so. But I didn't know. They kept me there for most of an hour, asking me over and over why I had done what I had done. They made it sound as though I could get out of trouble if I had a good reason, if I admitted it and said I was sorry. I have since come to know that this is just a tactic. Walmart always calls the police. But it didn't matter what tactics they used. I didn't understand them. I didn't understand myself. I didn't understand what was happening around me. Where was I again? And what was it they kept asking me about?

I became more and more panicked, more and more confused. I wanted to give them the answers they asked for, but I couldn't figure them out. I didn't *know* why I had stolen all that stuff.

I had to call my husband, Dave. But how did I tell him I was a thief? He thought I was a good person. Now, it was clear that I was not. Still, I picked up my phone and dialed Dave's number. He was on an airplane on his way to Denver, so obviously, he didn't answer. I pretended to talk to him anyway, just to give myself a break from the relentless questions of the man who sat across from me. I was still talking into my phone when suddenly the door to the tiny room opened and a police officer in full uniform stepped into the room. "Ma'am, put down your phone!" he shouted at me, and I almost dropped it in my haste to comply. "Now what do we have going on here?" he asked the security officer who sat across from me.

"A shoplifter," the man reported, "She won't tell us why or answer any questions. Just one more shoplifter who thinks they can get away with stealing."

The police officer was young, a man who looked new to the force. He wrote me a citation instructing me to appear in court the next day. Then they handed me the bags of things that had been on my receipt, the things I had paid for, and they sent me on my way. I stumbled out the door into the rain. It was late, after eleven and dark. I made it to my car. Or I must have, because the next thing I remember I was standing in my driveway, stumbling towards the house.

***

I don't remember much from that night after I left Walmart. Dave was out of town. I got home and got myself inside. I sat down on my bed, not getting ready to sleep, just rocking back and forth. I remember becoming aware of myself sitting on my bed as morning dawned. I had been awake all night, I think, though not particularly conscious. I was horrified and afraid. I had to appear in court that morning and enter a plea: guilty or not guilty. I didn't know which I was.

My mind was working well enough by then to piece together some of what had happened. I didn't understand why I had walked out of the store with half my cart unpaid for, but I did know I hadn't meant to do it. But did that matter? I had walked out and there was no question that I hadn't paid. So, did that mean I was guilty no matter what I'd intended to do?

My court appearance was set for 10am. I scrambled to my computer and googled lawyers in Missoula, the nearest town to our ranch. I poured through ads and names and finally just started at the top of the list and called everyone. On the sixth or seventh call, a man picked up. It was seven AM, in the morning. "Come right in," he told me. "I will meet with you as soon as you can get here."

I don't remember a lot about that meeting. I remember a big wooden table in a small office, and I must have told him my story. I explained that I had walked out of the store with a cart full of merchandise I hadn't bought. "But I think something is wrong. I have this illness … and I think something is wrong. I didn't mean to steal that stuff. But I clearly did. Does that mean I'm guilty?"

He was very clear that the statutes about theft required intention. If it was an accident—if somehow, I hadn't meant to do what I had done—then it wasn't theft according to the law. And in any case, he explained, I could always change my plea later. I would have months before the trial. If I had any doubt, I should plead not guilty and take some time to figure out what had happened.

I went immediately from his office to the big stone courthouse in downtown Missoula. It had marble floors and big wooden banisters. But the courtroom itself was a simple conference room, with two fold-up tables in the front. Dozens of people sat in the chairs at the back of the room, waiting for their names to be called. When mine was called, I made my way to the front of the room. "Ma'am," I asked the judge, "Is it allowed, am I allowed to ask to sit down for this? I have an illness that makes it difficult for me to stand for very long…"

"Of course," she said and waved to the bailiff, "bring her a chair, please."

She probably read something. I don't remember. I remember being uncomfortable in my dress. I never wore dresses anymore. I remember pleading not guilty and walking out of the courtroom, feeling like everyone had really been quite civil.

***

I spent the next two days in a daze, mostly sitting in my room in shock, trying to figure out what had happened. Dave and I talked every day, but I didn't tell him anything. I made excuses to get off the phone. I couldn't bring myself to tell him what I had done. I was so ashamed. I was so confused. I went back through the past few weeks trying to piece together what I had done each day. And what I found was appalling. I would remember driving to town to do a little shopping, maybe pick up some groceries, and then starting to get tired. Not tired like a normal person. Tired like my whole body was fighting through molasses. And then the blackouts began. I'd find myself at home with no memory of how I got there. Or back in my car in some parking lot staring at bags from four different stores, only able to remember one of them. And somehow the confusion that surrounded all these events was such that I never fully realized how wrong something must be. I pushed and pushed and found myself at home at last. I dropped into bed until I got up and did it all again. And I'd never seen what was going on.

But now, sitting at home with a charge of shoplifting and a court date, it became clear. Something was really wrong. Wrong with my brain, I mean. I knew it was connected to the fatigue, so I started doing research on Chronic Fatigue Syndrome to see if anyone else could explain it. And they could.

***

Things had changed in the field of Chronic Fatigue Syndrome since I had first been diagnosed with this illness. The CDC was forced to give the research money back to the Chronic Fatigue researchers and, what do you know, they actually learned things. This led to more research and over the course of a decade, Chronic Fatigue Syndrome (now sometimes called Myalgic Encephalomyelitis or CFS/ME) was becoming much more thoroughly understood. There were tests which could be used as diagnostic tools, a thorough understanding of the progression of the disease and a number of very promising treatment options, none of which I knew anything about.

The field was still small enough that none of my doctors knew anything about the new research, either. I was still the leading CFS/ME expert on my treatment team. But extensive information was becoming available. There were four or five research centers around the globe which were leading the world in CFS/ME research and treatment options. And they had come up with an understanding of how this illness typically progressed in late-stage cases.

I didn't know there was such a thing as "late-stage cases" or that this illness would be any different after twenty years than it was after ten. I didn't know that serious cases, as they progressed, were known to do damage to various organ systems, including the nervous system and the brain. I knew I had tremors in my hands and facial tics when my fatigue got bad, but I had no idea the damage that it was doing to my cognitive abilities.

As I read the latest research, I slowly pieced together what had happened the day of the shoplifting fiasco. I'd dropped Dave off at the airport, then gone into town to do some shopping. I had a list of four places I wanted to go. I must have gone to each of them, given all the stuff I had in my car, but I don't remember most of it. The exhaustion had hit early. By the time I got to Walmart and started my grocery shopping I was a mess. I think I wandered Walmart for hours, putting more and more stuff in my cart. I remember that one moment I would know what I was doing and try to continue my shopping and the next I would be standing there terrified, with no idea where I was or what was going on around me. Once I dropped some eyeliner on the floor and the thought of the energy it would take to bend down and pick it up had me almost in tears. I left it on the floor and walked on.

At some level, I must have known that something was very wrong because I remember turning a corner and seeing a woman I knew; and being totally overcome with relief. I was preparing to throw myself at her and cry out for help when I realized the woman was not who I thought she was. I didn't know her after all. I fell away from her even more confused than before. I could no longer remember why I thought I had needed help or what I had thought was wrong.

I put off going to the checkout lane because every time I thought of leaving the store I thought of driving home and some part of me knew I shouldn't be doing that. But I didn't know what to do instead. Eventually I knew that I was nearing a collapse and that if I didn't get out of that store soon, I was going to pass out right there. If that happened, someone would call an ambulance and I would be taken to the hospital. Even with insurance, the bills would be huge and there was nothing the hospital could do for me anyway. I could feel it coming on and knew that I had only a matter of minutes before I'd be unconscious. All I could think of was that I needed to get out of there now.

I chose the self-checkout lane because that's what I always did. Some of the items I must have paid for, because at the end I had a receipt. I only remember a few moments of the checkout process. I remember standing there with some object in my hand, suddenly having no idea what I was supposed to be doing with it. In the end, I reached a moment where all I knew was that I had to get to the car right now and I dropped everything back into my cart and left the store, cart, and all. That's when I was stopped.

As I spent the next few days processing through what had happened, I tried to understand how I could have let things get this bad. How had I gotten into this situation? It started with a cure.

***

Nine months earlier…

I was 45 years old, owned an off-grid horse ranch in the mountains of Montana and I had just spent six hours riding my horse through the mountains with friends. Dusty, and dry from the trail, I was grinning as I brushed down my sweaty mare. I looked up and caught sight of Dave coming down to the barn with a tray filled with glasses of lemonade.

"I thought you guys might need this," he told us as he handed out the drinks, following them up with sandwiches, cut diagonally the way I liked. "That was a long ride!"

Everyone cheered as I kissed his cheek. "You are my hero," I told him.

Later that evening we sat around the campfire, finishing up the dinner we had cooked and drinking lightly with those same friends. The sun went down, and the stars came up, covering our sky with beauty from horizon to horizon. Eventually someone suggested we all head to bed. I didn't want to. I wasn't tired. But they were right, it was late. I let myself be led inside, glowing with happiness.

***

For the first time since I was a teenager, I wasn't sick. Two weeks ago, my life-long illness had gone away, just like that, leaving me energetic and ready to live the life I wanted for the first time since I was sixteen years old.

I have ADD. This is very common for people with CFS/ME, it turns out. A high proportion of the CFS/ME population also has ADD.

Most often, my ADD was an asset to me. ADD isn't all inattention. The flip side of it is that when you come across something you love, you have the ability to hyper-focus on it and accomplish far more than most people could in that situation. I loved learning and it allowed me to throw myself into school and accomplish great things despite a memory-related learning disability and an illness which fought to slow me down. But it did take me twelve hours to write a paper that should have taken three, and organizing my office was next to impossible: Until I discovered Ritalin. On Ritalin, I was efficient and effective without losing any of my creative edge. I took it often in college, and occasionally after, when I had a project to do that required extra focus.

***

I'd lived in Montana for about twelve years, and I had finally come to some real peace about my illness and my life. I fought exhaustion every day, rarely able to ride my horses more than an hour or two at a time. I couldn't ride my horses and then spend time with people in the evenings, because I was too exhausted to do more than one thing in a day. But that was the way my life had been for decades now. And the truth was, I had a really good life. I had a husband I loved, a ranch I loved and animals coming out of my ears. I didn't have kids of my own, but I was close to my four nieces and spent a lot of time with them when I could.

I was no longer searching for a cure. I was living with what I had. I was blessed.

Over the years I had come to find a great deal of peace in that. As I moved into my forties, I found, for the first time in my life, that I wasn't fighting to do what I couldn't do. I was—mostly—content with what I had.

During a routine appointment, one of my doctors suggested I try Vyvanse, a Ritalin alternative. I took it the next time I needed to focus and overnight my fatigue went away.

It just went away. I woke up the next morning and felt good, like I was rested and full of energy. I hadn't felt that way in decades. The heavy weight of my body was gone. I felt like I could fly. Suddenly it was clear to me how much I had been missing because suddenly I had it all back.

Just like that, I wasn't tired anymore. For the first time in my adult life, I woke up full of energy, worked all day and could still enjoy supper with friends in the evening. I went on 15-mile horseback rides. I expanded my business, ramping up my horse breeding program and offered riding lessons on the side. Everything I'd ever dreamed of doing with the ranch, I did.

It was like being born into a whole new world to experience life unfettered for the first time. To get up in the morning, work all day and still be capable of going out with friends that evening was a revelation to me. On my best days, I had never approached this. I was euphoric.

I was also aware that I was not being fair to Dave. For fifteen years, he had done the dishes, handled the grocery shopping, cleaned the house, and taken care of me while I was sick. For fifteen years, he had done all the work of our lives in order to leave me able to use what little energy I had for the things I loved. And when suddenly I had as much energy as he, did I step up and take back my share—helping with the dishes and making dinner and doing the laundry? I did not.

It wasn't that I wasn't aware of the need to do these things. The truth was, after fifteen years of doing all of the work in both of our lives, Dave was exhausted. And it had been a long time since he had had time to spend on things he enjoyed. I knew this. And I fully intended to take back my half of the work. I just couldn't do it yet.

All my life I had dreamed of doing so many things which now—suddenly—I could do. I needed, I *needed*, to revel in that. Not forever. A month, maybe two. And then I would have gotten my fill, met all the desperate, angry cravings that cried to please, please, *please*, let me hike this mountain, ride this horse, teach this class, lead this seminar. Let me go out to dinner, get together with friends, talk about politics, religion, and life and to live, live, *live*. Eventually, two months at most, I would have filled that screaming, crying need and I would have leveled out, taken up my share of things, given Dave his break. I almost told him so, almost explained to him that I could see he needed his break as much as I needed my living but just give me two months and I will give it to you, take up my responsibilities and settle down. But I was too busy, too lost in the euphoria of living a life with energy and I kept hoping that my need, my insatiable *need*, would ease and he would see that I had not forgotten him…

And that might have happened. But after two months, the medicine stopped working.

***

13

It just stopped. It was August, nearing the end of my summer full of energy and over the course of a week, the fatigue came back with a vengeance. We upped the dosage, but we couldn't get it to work again. It turned out that the new medicine had been taking energy from my adrenal system just like Ritalin did and in doing so, it had damaged them almost beyond repair. The new medicine had done extensive damage to all my systems, and not only was all my progress gone, but I was worse than I had ever been before. And I couldn't accept it.

All that peace I had found? Gone. All that acceptance and willingness to focus on what I had? Gone. I had seen what life would have been like without this illness and I could not accept those limitations anymore.

Not that I had a choice. The limitations were back and there was nothing I could do about them. Or almost nothing. In fact, there was one thing I could do, and I did it with a vengeance. I could fight.

I fought. I refused to rest, I refused to slow down. I pushed on despite screaming pain and screamed right back. I pushed until I collapsed and then I got up screaming and did it all again. I was *angry*. I was taking stupid risks. I was miserable. I barely knew where I was from one minute to the next. But I *would not* slow down. And when Dave, who watched me live my dreams for two months and never once stop to take the load off his shoulders, tried to tell me he thought I was out of control, I took my anger out on him.

This was one of the few times in our marriage when we were truly at odds with each other. I was angry and my anger was spilling out all over Dave. This was not usual for me. I usually kept my emotions where they belonged, not taking things out on people who didn't deserve them. Certainly, not on Dave. But here I was, and I couldn't stop myself. I was angry at the world. Dave was the only part of the world I had access to, so I took it out on Dave.

Dave was overwhelmed, frustrated, and disappointed in me. I started spending money recklessly and we were rapidly filling up our credit cards. Dave was scared of how I was living. He tried to hold that all in, but it weighed heavy on him. He was angry at how I was treating him after all his years of service; angry that I was undoing all the financial progress we had made. I saw it, as out of the corner of my eye, but I could not stop myself.

I would come home having bought hundreds of dollars' worth of things that I had no memory of buying. Or I would collapse on a mountain trail an hour from the ranch and Dave would have to leave work to come get me, load up my horse and drive me home. Or I would drive to town and then become unable to sit up long enough to drive home and Dave would have to come get me, figuring out how to get the cars home as well. He tried to tell me. Over and over, he said he thought I was out of control. I was going to hurt someone. I was making a mess of my life.

He said it more nicely. But he was getting desperate because I wouldn't listen. I refused to stop. I was running up crazy bills and having close calls when driving. There were whole periods of each day I couldn't remember. But I refused to stop. I refused to give up one more thing to this illness. It wasn't fair. It simply wasn't fair.

***

I sat in my room in our little log cabin on our horse ranch in Montana and tried to understand what had happened to me that night at Walmart and more, what had been happening for months now. It was nine months since I had had the best summer of my life and less than a week since that night at Walmart.

Research now reveals that as CFS/ME progresses, patients with extreme cases (like mine) begin to experience "episodes" of confusion in which their brains don't process information correctly. They may not know where they are or who they are, and they may phase in and out of awareness every few minutes. They described it exactly—everything I experienced. And it turned out these episodes left damage to the brain which could be recorded and tracked, even down to the time frame in which they occurred. As I read about my own experiences in the medical literature, I came to realize that this had been happening for a while. I began to dig through my closet and find things I had bought both that day and over the past few weeks. I pulled out receipts and compared them to the purchases I had. Many didn't match.

In tears and some amount of hysteria, I tallied up everything I could find that had not been paid for and called every store on my list. There was a dress from Old Navy, a battery charger from Home Depot and some grooming tools from the local tack shop. I had receipts for other items bought at the same time, but not for them. Trying (somewhat unsuccessfully) not to cry, I asked to talk to managers and poured out my tale: I had just discovered that I had been having episodes in which I didn't know where I was or what was happening around me due to a worsening of an illness we hadn't realized had progressed to this point. I thought I had walked out of a number of stores without paying for things when this had happened and had identified X amount of dollars that I owed them. Should I bring the items back? Should I pay for them over the phone? Most of the stores accepted payment over the phone. Home Depot told me not to worry about it and just to keep the items for free. Everyone was kind and gentle and probably really wanted to get off the phone with the hysterical lady who was hardly making sense.

CHAPTER 2

All My Mistakes

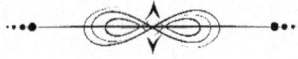

I Had met with a lawyer and gone to court, and I hadn't told Dave about any of it. Dave and I shared everything. In twelve years of marriage, we had always had each other's backs and lived life together, as partners. Until now. As I came out of the fog of those days, it slowly became clear to me that the real betrayal, the worst thing I'd done, was not tell Dave right away.

Weeks ago, Dave had started asking me about the endless bags I brought home, the endless money I was spending. "Do you know how much you spent today?" or "What did you buy at Target?" or "Were you *planning* on going to all of these places?"

I never had an answer for him. I didn't know how much I spent. I didn't know what I had bought. I not only hadn't planned to go those places; I hadn't realized I did until he pointed out the bags. Dave had always been extra careful not to ride me about money. I had never been well enough to work so all the money in our lives came from Dave's job. We had known things would be that way from the beginning. Not wanting to start our marriage out with a big discrepancy in power, we had both agreed long ago that all money was ours equally. But Dave was getting worried.

He was worried about a lot more than money, of course. He would meet me in the driveway and help me stumble into the house. I dropped my coat and purse and bags of goods the minute I walked through the door, then fell into bed, barely able to speak. When I'd wake up, he'd try to talk to me. "I don't think you were in good enough condition to be driving yesterday. You could barely speak when you got home. I just don't think you should be driving when you are like that..."

I lashed out at him. I shut him down. "I'm fine," Or "Next time I'll rest in the car before I come home," or "I was tired when I got home but I can manage while I have to." That summer I had felt what it was like to live without fetters. Now that the limits had come back, I refused to accept them. And I was angry. So, I ignored Dave. I ignored him even though I could see his rising panic, his anger, his frustration.

So, Dave was in Denver, and I was in Montana. It was three days after the Walmart night. Finally, I called and told him about it. I don't remember what I said, but Dave was floored. Not as much by what had happened as by my keeping it from him for so long. We'd talked every day and I had not told him any of it. He had already been panicked, watching my life self-destruct (and his along with it) while I refused to listen to his warnings or his pleas. Now he felt betrayed. How had I not called him first? The very moment things went wrong. How had I visited lawyers and gone to court and kept it all from him?

In retrospect, that was the biggest indicator that I was still not in my right mind, still not thinking clearly. To have done all this without telling Dave was a betrayal I would never have made if my brain was working right. But I had made it. And it took Dave months to get over the betrayal he felt, come to terms with his anger and let it go. It took months for him to find his way out of you-made-this-mess-you-deal-with-it and I-told-you-so and stand by my side once again.

So, there we were on the phone, as I told him all that had happened, all that I had kept from him. Dave was angry, blown away and in shock. I was half hysterical, trying to tell him about events I barely remembered or could make sense of. At one point, I told him that I thought I had been driving a lot lately when I was in this state and had no memory of it. I said that I was lucky I had not hurt anyone. And he said, "How do you know you didn't?

You don't remember driving home. How do you know you didn't hit someone with your car and just not notice?" And I lost it.

It was like someone had punched me in the gut. I dropped into full blown hysterics. He was right. How did I know I hadn't *killed* someone while I was driving home from Walmart that night and just didn't remember it?

All at once it was very real to me, what I could have done. Two of my nieces lived in Missoula. Every time I drove, I had risked not just some nameless stranger but *them*, two of the most important people in my world. In my mind, I saw it over and over, *their* destruction. *Their* lives taken. And what did it matter if it hadn't been them? In this state of mind, I could have killed anyone, destroying families, destroying lives. And maybe I had. How would I know?

I hung up on Dave. I called the police. Hysterically, I stumbled through an explanation. We'd just discovered I'd been having episodes of driving when I was unaware of what was going on around me and I said, "Thank goodness I didn't hurt anyone," and my husband said, "How do you know you didn't hurt anyone?" and I realized I could have hurt someone and not remembered it and did they have any reports of hit and runs on the night in question or damage done along the route I was driving?"

My voice was shrill, and I was gasping for air. The officer told me to calm down. "Is there any damage to your car?" he asked. I ran out and looked. No. No damage at all. "Then you aren't likely to have hit anything," he told me, and proceeded to check his records for the route and the time. He assured me that nothing was reported, and he was sure it was fine.

***

Over the next couple of weeks, I pieced together what had happened and slowly came to be able to think clearly again. And I mulled over what to do. Dave stood on the sidelines and watched. He wanted to support me, but he was hurt, confused and angry.

I got medical tests and gathered information from experts. I made my case to explain myself. I wasn't sure if I was going to use these things to argue my innocence. I didn't feel innocent, and I was committed to doing what was right, no matter if it was the best thing for *me* or not.

Dave's observations about the potential destruction I could have caused with my driving had changed everything. They had changed me. I was convinced that I had *not* hurt anyone but somehow that didn't lift the punch-in-the-gut realization that I *could* have. How close I had come. How lucky I was. While part of me gathered information in my defense, a greater part of me no longer cared if I was convicted or not. I felt like I had dodged a bullet. I was so filled with gratitude that things had not been worse, so thankful that *something* had gotten my attention before I killed someone and had to live with *that* for the rest of my life, that being convicted of shoplifting seemed a small price to pay compared to what might have been. And though I had not intended to shoplift, the truth was, it never would have happened if I had been acting like a responsible adult rather than an angry child. I had chosen to indulge my anger. I had refused to slow down. A person could be responsible for a death because they made bad decisions even if they didn't mean to kill anyone. Maybe it was the same with shoplifting?

The thing was, I didn't trust my own judgment anymore. I didn't know how to decide what to do. Did I keep my not guilty plea or change it to guilty? I was gathering evidence to explain myself, but did I even want to use it? Did I deserve this conviction or not?

I didn't know how to decide. How could I judge my own competence? Everything felt so unsure. What could I rely on and what could I not and how was I to know?

And if I couldn't rely on my own judgment, who could advise me? Who could tell me what the right thing to do was? When I talked to my family about it, they were clearly trying to protect me. Dave was still too upset himself to see any of this clearly. I could ask a lawyer, but it was a lawyer's job to protect me too. I wanted to do what was *right*. Who would have the expertise to know what was right in this situation?

I called the county prosecutor whose job it was to prosecute me for shoplifting.

"Listen," I said. "I am going to tell you a story. I know you have no reason to believe it but set that aside for a moment. We can deal with that later. For now, I need to know, *if* you believed this story were true, what would you want me to do?" He listened. He said, "You are right, I have no reason to believe it just by hearing your word. But I also have no desire to prosecute someone who doesn't deserve it. Gather all the evidence you can and send it to me. And beyond that, it's a judgement of character. If your evidence is strong and I believe you are someone who is telling me the truth, I will drop the charges."

So, that's what I did. For three months, I gathered medical data and asked for letters of character reference from friends, college professors, ministers, and community leaders. The day of the trial the prosecutor called me into his office and told me he was dismissing the charges. He said he was sorry these things were happening to me and wished me the best of luck. I left with tears in my eyes and cried in Dave's arms when we got home.

***

Shortly after the Walmart incident, I had the worst crash of my life. It was like, after all that pain and stress, my body just fell apart. It lasted for three years with some times better and some times worse but no times good. Most of the time I was so exhausted I couldn't even sit up, much less stand. I spent three years recovering, spending hours each day in bed and needing a wheelchair whenever we left the house. I had trouble sitting up long enough to eat dinner with my family. The brain fog I had been experiencing now and then became a permanent state. I struggled to find my words and often couldn't hold a simple conversation. I couldn't go anywhere alone because I couldn't think clearly enough to understand where I was at any given moment, and I was prone to collapsing without warning.

I lay in bed for weeks, then months at a time and all my mistakes, all my failures gathered around me. I was too worn down to be bored. I was beaten, lost. I prayed for life to just be over, for this never-ending struggle to finally, finally end. But it didn't end. Instead, as I lay there, my life came back to me in waves, and I found myself sorting through all that had brought me to this place.

Section Two

Adventuring

19 years old - 27 years old...

Life is either a daring adventure or nothing.

(Helen Keller)

CHAPTER 3

College

"I'd call what you have more of a lupoid type arthritis than straight Rheumatoid Arthritis. And compared to most of my patients you are doing quite well."

The doctor, middle aged with thinning hair, was sitting on a stool across from me. I was on the exam table, in his office in downtown St. Paul, in one of those flimsy hospital gowns that never seemed to stay shut. I had just finished my monthly exam with the Rheumatologist near my college. "But I'm exhausted all the time," I said, "and I can hardly keep up with my classes. I'm in pain every day. I can't see how I'm going to manage to hold a job. What can we do about that?"

He looked surprised. "I don't think you ever will hold a job. This is a serious illness. It's unlikely you will be able to finish school, much less work afterwards. But you are doing great compared to most people with this illness. I'd say be happy with what you've got while you have it."

I don't think you ever will hold a job. It's unlikely you will be able to finish school, much less work afterwards.

I was numb as I dressed and walked out of the exam room. There was a hollow feeling in the pit of my stomach I couldn't identify. The world felt unreal around me.

I don't think you ever will hold a job. It's unlikely you will be able to finish school, much less work afterwards.

24

I got on the bus and stared out the window on my way back to school. The hollow feeling had moved from my stomach to my whole body. It vibrated inside me. The bus pulled up to the local mall, about halfway between my doctor's office and my school. Suddenly I jumped up and ran off the bus. It was ridiculous. I didn't need anything at the mall. I never shopped at malls, anyway, preferring to get my clothes from secondhand stores like Goodwill. Besides, clothes had never really mattered to me all that much. And I had no money. What was I doing at the mall?

I walked the mall until I found it. A fancy women's clothing shop. Something with prom dresses and ball gowns. I went inside.

I was looking for a dress. An elegant dress. A red dress. I saw the one I wanted and the strangled feeling which gripped my throat began to ease. My breath eased. The tension in my body evaporated and I stood straighter, my shoulders relaxing as my hand ran over the satiny fabric of the dress. This dress was everything I needed. It was beauty incarnate. It was freedom. It was power and confidence and strength. It was elegance and desirability and success. No one who owned a dress like this had to fear their body. No one who owned a dress like this had their lives taken away by weakness, exhaustion, and pain.

Never mind that I never went anywhere such a dress could be worn. Never mind that they were out of the dress in my size, so I had to buy one that was too small. The dress was $400. I had a credit card my parents had gotten me for emergencies. It had a $500 limit. I bought the dress.

I was a person who owned a dress like this—a person with strength and power and confidence. A person with her whole life ahead of her who was free to be everything she dreamed of being. As I wrapped the dress in its carry sack, I was flooded with joy. My whole body rang with the excitement, the promise I saw laid out before me. I loved this life with a passion I could hardly contain.

As I rode home from the mall I tapped my foot in excitement. I rushed to my dorm, almost forgetting about the dress already, and hung it in the back of my closet. I ran out to meet up with some friends. "How was your doctor's appointment?" one of them asked. I was surprised. I had forgotten all about it. "It was great!" I laughed, and we went about our day.

Ten years later I came across that dress. Next to it were three others. A ball gown, a fancy silk cocktail dress, all of them red, all of them hundreds of dollars. I stared in confusion at the dresses. What were these doing here? I remembered, barely, buying each one. None of them fit me anymore. My body had changed; I had gained weight as I neared thirty. Each of these dresses still hung in the plastic dress bag it had come in. I had never worn any of them.

***

I didn't apply to any second-choice colleges. I knew that I could get in anywhere I wanted to go. I considered Harvard, Brown and American University in Washington D.C. Harvard I wanted to go to for graduate school, not undergraduate. The others I may have been interested in, but I went to visit Macalester College in St. Paul, Minnesota, and the minute I stepped on the campus, I knew. This was my school.

I'd been valedictorian of my High School class. I'd gotten a scholarship from the United States Congress to spend a year as an exchange student in Germany and had lived there the year the Berlin Wall came down. I'd had the leading role in every school play my school put on and helped design a peer helping program for Iowa schools, a program overseen by the governor. My grades were near perfect, my test scores high. I was an accomplished public speaker and a good writer. My life was laid out before me and glowed with potential. Except there was this illness. Juvenile Rheumatoid Arthritis. Joint pain, exhaustion. My doctors told me to slow down, rest more, not push myself so hard. I ignored them. I refused to let anything get in the way of the life that I loved.

26

***

College, the first year, was a fight with an opponent I couldn't see. I played the college game and lived the college life. Bedtime at 2 a.m., all-night conversations in the lounge and exciting weekends exploring campus and freedom. I would try to get rest, take a nap every day, eat the right foods and ask for extensions on assignments when my arthritis got bad. But in the face of 1200 'normal' college students the unreality of it all came back full force.

I was tired. But what was tired?

"Are you sure you're not just depressed?"

"The problem is you're sleeping too much. Just get up and do things and you'll feel fine."

"You have to force yourself to do exercise. You only think it exhausts you because you aren't doing it enough. Force yourself to exercise and it will give you energy."

"You're tired? Aren't we all! I was up until 2 a.m. last night and I got up at 6 for volleyball practice. I could fall asleep right now!"

What is 'tired'? Nothing tangible enough to be understood at twenty, but tangible enough indeed, to fight and rage against. And I had begun to fight.

I woke up every day with this joy singing in my heart, unable to stop smiling, loving every minute I was alive. And so, when my body hurt, when it screamed out in pain at the exhaustion I felt, I ignored it. What's more, I didn't believe it. I was too strong a person to be taken down by something as petty as my physical body. I pushed on.

A week, perhaps, of pushing myself like this and I would collapse in a heap on the floor. Then the pain was bad enough to trust, the exhaustion was complete and the opponent I was fighting was clear and as real as my bones. I was sick. I was really sick and there was nothing I could do to change it.

Relieved, I would put myself to bed, no guilt to stop me, and rest in comfort. While my roommate bopped in and out at all hours of the day and night I lay, sleeping like the dead. A few days later I would start the cycle again.

* * *

My second year of college, I was waffling between denying and believing in this illness. That finally began to pass. It passed because my health had become so bad that my opponent was always visible. And it passed because the outside voices had stopped questioning whether the problems were real. "There's nothing wrong with you," had become replaced by a startled look and "Christie, you don't look so good." Strangers on the street had begun to stop and asked if I were all right. My hair was limp, and I had gone from nicely thin to gaunt. I look gray, they said, and only half alive. But still, I fought.

I was five foot six, thin and good looking, and I had learned to wear make-up and flattering clothes, despite never caring much about such things. I loved life. I loved learning. I threw myself into each of my classes and every opportunity that came along. I was appointed to the campus Judicial committee, and I spent hours staying up until 3 or 4 a.m. to decide a case I had chaired. I was involved in almost every case between students, faculty or staff and almost every time I was involved the dean asked me to chair the committee, to be both moderator and a member of the 'jury'.

I took a job as a Resident's Assistant on the new 'Women's Issues Floor' and I spent the year walking students through the aftermath of rape, the discovery of childhood abuse, the decision to get an abortion, or not, as well as all of the major and minor school or personal crisis which college students experience.

I took as many classes as I was allowed, and I did my best to hold together all the requirements of a double major. I had long wanted to go into politics, setting my sights on Harvard Law School. I studied Political Science

28

and Philosophy, took classes in Anthropology and Psychology. I wanted to learn everything, and I wanted, someday, to spend my life changing the world.

I knew our world was broken. I watched as the U.S. government funded dictators in third world countries in order to keep American prices down. I saw people all around me fighting for their basic rights: gays, African Americans, women. I knew we could do better, and I had long ago decided that I would spend my life fixing those things that were broken. It was how I dealt with the crushing weight I had felt when, as a teenager, I had become aware of all the pain and suffering in the world. Yes, there was pain. Yes, there was suffering. But I would change it. I would change it all.

* * *

I volunteered at a homeless shelter, worked two jobs, and took every class I could. And my body struggled. The more I ignored it, the worse it became. In the midst of all this, I had been re-diagnosed with Lupus, as the doctors searched for a better explanation for the destruction that my body was doing to itself. I was told I might have to go on anti-chemotherapy drugs, was always in pain, and didn't know what it was like not to be exhausted. Lupus was a much more serious illness than Rheumatoid Arthritis. Like RA, Lupus occurs when the immune system, which normally helps protect the body from infection and disease, attacks its own tissue. This attack causes inflammation, and in some cases, permanent tissue damage, which can be widespread—affecting the skin, joints, heart, lung, kidneys, circulating blood cells, and brain.

I had taken to passing out suddenly from exhaustion and would sometimes stay largely unconscious for days at a time. I was usually semi-conscious for a number of hours after collapsing and would spend that time lying where I had fallen, wondering if I would die there, railing at all the limits of my body. I once blacked out on my way home from the library at two AM in the middle of a Minnesota January on a night with a wind-chill of seventy below. I remember clearly the fight to stay conscious and the last few seconds

29

in which I felt the blackness overtake me and registered that I was still a block from home. I remember my last thought being a rational realization that I was going to die in this snow, and then I lost consciousness. I remember waking up in my own bed shortly after collapsing, having been carried there by a friend who had followed me out of the library that night.

CHAPTER 4

Colorado and Andy

It was too much. Just too much. I had been fighting to do all the things I wanted to do and all the fighting did was grind my body down. By the end of my sophomore year, I could no longer attend classes. I could barely stand up. It finally got through to me. This life was killing me. I had to stop. I had to leave college and give myself time to heal.

Once I knew that I couldn't return to college, I decided that I would move to Colorado to be with my boyfriend, Andy. Andy was in his senior year at Colorado State University, and we would get an apartment together in Fort Collins. I was devastated by leaving school.

After high school, I had worked at a summer camp in Colorado. It had been a struggle to keep up with the intense pace of the job and I had barely made it through the summer there. I had hoped to return to this camp each year between college. It was where I had met Andy. I loved the kids, the mountains, and the horses I rode. I loved everything about it. But that summer I didn't return to camp. Pushing myself to manage was no longer an option. I could hardly even stand up. I moved with Andy into a small, one bedroom apartment on the edge of Fort Collins. I would spend time recovering from the toll the last years had taken on my body and focus on studying ways different cultures had treated auto-immune diseases throughout history. I'd designed an independent study with a professor at Macalester to study this. I knew by that point that medical science had nothing to offer me in terms of a cure and only little in terms of treatment. But I didn't believe that this half life I was living could possibly be my life forever. I had too many dreams, too much potential, too much to *offer* the world. Surely it couldn't be my fate to lose all that, to spend my life in bed, unable to give all I had to give to a world that needed it so much.

I was sure there was an answer out there. I just had to find it. So, I researched Traditional Chinese Medicine, Native American journeying, and herbal traditions from all over the world. I studied spiritual healing and everything else I could find. I would lie in bed and Andy would bring me books, picking up new books from his school's library as needed. I would struggle to sit up, often propping myself up on pillows as much as I could and writing in the notebooks spread out around me. It was exhausting to hold a pen. Every few minutes I would lay my pen down and rest.

Through all of this, Andy took care of me, paying the bills and cooking our meals and making sure my needs were met. I slept and I studied, and I felt every moment how grateful I was for this generous man who made me laugh and helped me through my days.

***

Before moving to Colorado, I called the summer camp we had worked at and asked them if I could take one of their horses for the off-season. They often let staff members do this, as their horses spent most of the year running wild in winter pasture and a horse that was cared for and ridden all year was a lot easier to get ready for campers in the spring. I wanted a horse called Bluebar whom I had ridden the year before. But I couldn't remember its name or even if it had been a male or female. I just knew that it had been a striped-back-dun, with a golden body, black mane and tail and a dark dorsal stripe down its back. The year before, camp had two horses that matched that description: Bluebar and Two-Bits. One was a solid, trustworthy horse I had ridden often and the other I didn't know well.

Buebar had been sold to an eager camper. I called the camp to ask about the horse I wanted, and they suggested that it might be Two-Bits. I agreed. I made arrangements to take her with me to Fort Collins and board her there.

It isn't that I thought I would be able to ride much. At the time, I made the arrangements, I could barely sit up in bed without help. But it wasn't just about the riding. I was drawn to horses. I wanted the relationship more than anything. Oh, I lived for riding. But even without that, I wanted to *know* a horse. And my family felt that it might be important for me to have something special that was just my own, something to care for and love during this time when I was sick and needed so much care myself, so they helped me pay for her care.

I spent the summer mostly in bed, while Two-Bits worked at camp. I was recovering from the worst of the exhaustion. In the fall, as my energy slowly began to improve, Two-Bits was moved to Fort Collins and I started spending time with her. In the mornings, when Andy left the house for class, he would drive me over to Two-Bits' pasture and leave me with a blanket and a brown bag lunch. Sometimes I would bring a book I was reading, usually something about some obscure healing tradition that promised to make me well. Sometimes I brought books on medicinal herbs and studied the plants around where I lay. The pasture was just off a busy road, but I would trudge as far back from the road as I could get. I would spread out my blanket in the back of her pasture and lay all day watching Two-Bits graze. She was striking with compact, quarter horse muscles and rounded hips. When something excited her, her head came up, her nostrils flared, and her neck arched. She looked like a goddess in that field. She was pure power and strength. She was health.

At first, she ignored me. Two-Bits had been a racehorse, and racehorses are rarely treated well. Their lives are harsh and their people tough. Two-Bits had no use for people. People were untrustworthy instruments of stress and pain. She ignored me, expecting me to walk the pasture any time I wanted to put a halter on her, expecting me to come to her. But I didn't. I couldn't chase after her. I was too weak. I found my spot in her pasture and settled in to wait.

Over the weeks as I lay in that pasture things began to change. At first the changes were small. Two-Bits started out grazing all day with her back to me, showing disdain in a very horsey way—by refusing even to acknowledge my existence. But as days passed and I asked nothing of her, she began to turn, just a little, to watch me out of the corner of her eye. Eventually she began to stand fully facing me, watching me openly as I entered her pasture and set myself up for the day. When, after settling my blanket in a corner of the pasture one day, I walked to her, she stood, tense and nose flared but not moving. She let me come.

I started by running my hands over her back. Then I left her and settled myself on my blanket, asking no more of her than that. After a few days of this, I began practicing the massage techniques I was learning. I had gotten a book on horse massage so that I could interact with her even though I was too weak to ride yet. Soon I would stand for as long as I could, massaging her muscles and rubbing her favorite spots before I sat. After that she would graze near me for the rest of the day.

Eventually, when I pulled up in the morning she would be standing at the gate, her head pointed towards me, ears alert. She would watch me shuffle into her pasture and painstakingly lay out my blanket, put down my books and my lunch, and turn to greet her, waiting for me to run my hands over her hard body and begin my morning massage. I felt her pain and her distrust of people. And I felt as it slowly began to give way to the possibility that *I* was different. To a horse, connection is everything. She needed it as much as I did. And slowly, she began allowing herself to get it. She was power and strength, and yet, as she finally began to trust me, she vibrated with vulnerability. She was a wonder to me.

As the winter progressed and my days laying in her pasture continued, my body finally began to heal. I could stand for longer and longer. I could slip a halter over her head and lead her on walks around the neighborhood. Then, finally, I could ride.

34

Only I could hardly ride her at all.

She was far too advanced a horse for me. But, being new to horses, I didn't realize how out of my league she was. I groomed her up, placed the saddle on her back and tried to get on.

Two-Bits had been taught to take off at a gallop the minute a foot hit her stirrup. I didn't know how to teach her differently and I struggled to get on. It took hours sometimes and I would be exhausted when I finally found myself clinging to her back, feet in the stirrups, fighting to keep her from running away with me. Every ride was a fight. It was everything I could do to keep her from running me to my death. Often, we would end our rides with her frustrated and confused and me exhausted and dispirited.

But every now and then we would have a good day, a day when I could control her, and we rode among the mountain lakes and foothill trails on the outskirts of Fort Collins. She would stretch her long, powerful legs and show me her world like a proud child. And I would come back elated, high for days from that one ride.

* * *

As my energy improved, I rode her every chance I got. On days when I couldn't get out there, I craved her, wished to be with her and dreamed of her. I was twenty years old, and I was weak and tired. I felt dull and drab. My promise leaked away into rumpled sheets and flattened pillows. All that I prided myself on was gone. Except her.

She was my legs. On her back I could get to the wilderness I loved. She was my breath. With her lungs, I could run, hooves thundering down dirt trails, muscles straining, mane blowing in the wind. She was my pride. While people looked on me with pity, my gray face and my limp hair, when I was on her back, they watched me with wonder and envy as I danced on lightening and shown with energy and power.

35

***

For the first four or five months of living together, living with Andy was wonderful. We sat quietly in the evenings watching TV or we went next door to where a group of his friends lived in another apartment. A few times a week we hung out with them. We played card games and watched superhero movies. I would always get tired after a couple of hours and we would go home together, content.

I had told Andy from the start that I didn't want to get married, just never saw myself doing that. I had rarely met a man who didn't make me feel less free, less able to achieve my dreams when I was with him than when I was alone. So, I had long ago determined that I preferred being alone. I would date for a time, but I always knew that dating would only go so far. I saw no reason to get married. I didn't want kids and I'd told him that I would let him know if that ever changed. I knew he felt differently about it.

But as we built a life together in our little apartment on the edge of Fort Collins, something began to shift. I had never felt like this before, so close to a person, so in love. He was there for me when I needed him most. Yes, there were some problems. He resisted buying the organic food I felt my body needed because it was so much more expensive. He preferred ready-made snacks and processed food. But it was his money we were spending. I couldn't complain too much. I hadn't known there could be a relationship this strong. The term *girlfriend* just didn't fit. I was more than just his girlfriend. I was his partner. And I wanted the words we used for each other to reflect that. I was ready to take the next step. I thought that must mean marriage. So, I told him I had changed my mind. I would consider marriage after all. That was surely what these feelings meant. That was surely the next step I was looking for.

I told him as we cooked dinner together one night in our little kitchen with the window overlooking the parking lot. I was ready to get married. We didn't discuss it much. The next night, as we were walking along a small pond behind our apartment, he got down on one knee and proposed. He didn't have a ring, but he put his heart into it. I was suffused with happiness. My life couldn't have been more perfect at that moment.

We told our families and took engagement pictures. We talked to the camp about using their chapel for our wedding. My energy was coming back, and life was looking up in all ways. But as my strength began to grow, so did my discontent.

At first, I was happy to spend our free evenings sitting in front of the TV. I had energy for little else, after all. But as my energy returned, so did my passion for life. I wanted to be active, get out of the house. And mostly I wanted the TV to be off. I hated that constant suck at my attention. I wanted to do things or talk about things or learn things. I wanted to go hiking, ride my horse and watch the sunset. Andy enjoyed spending time with his friends but when we weren't with them, he mostly just wanted to watch TV. And he didn't understand why suddenly I wasn't content with that.

But I wasn't. And I became less and less content the healthier I got.

* * *

I had two friends come and stay with me that winter. Just short stays. A weekend, and a week. Andy resented them. They took my time away from him and made our lives more hectic. I wanted hectic. I wanted passionate discussions about the world. I wanted to drive up into the mountains. I wanted evenings with the TV off. But I found their visits stressful, with Andy angry and resentful all the time. I tried to talk to him about it, but Andy didn't like to be confronted with problems. He treated each issue I brought up as a personal attack. He couldn't accept that people have faults, and their faults don't have to define them. If I had a complaint, it meant he wasn't good enough, that I didn't love him. It was exhausting and frustrating. My resentment grew.

Andy resented not just my friends but the things I loved to do without him. Not that I wouldn't have been happy to have him join me. But he didn't want to. He wanted to sit on the couch and watch TV or play video games with his friends. He just wanted me to want that too.

Eventually I couldn't hide my misery any longer. I wanted to engage in life in a way that Andy never would. He was content with things the way they were. I struggled to understand why I was so unhappy and to explain it to him and to myself.

I loved Andy but it all came down to this: This was not the man I wanted to marry. It wasn't just his watching TV or my love of hiking. Those were easy symbols of a deeper truth. Andy was content to let life happen, to let life unfold largely unexamined and unchallenged. I was not. I wanted to understand, to search, and to know every thought, every feeling I experienced in this world. And I wanted my partner to join me, at least some of the time, on those adventures too. And the truth was, Andy hated that. He could not challenge himself without turning the challenge into criticism. And because of that, he detested self-examination. He could not look at himself and see anything but flaws, and he naturally assumed that anyone else would see the same. He did not see my examinations as interesting adventures. He saw them as attacks. My attempts to live an examined life weren't just uninteresting to him. They were threatening. He wanted me to stop. What he never understood was that I couldn't stop. This kind of inner exploration was so central to who I was that the only way to separate it from me was to deny an essential part of myself. This had been easy when I was too tired, too exhausted to string two thoughts together. But as I came back to myself, it became harder and, eventually, impossible.

CHAPTER 5

Falling And Being Found

It came to me finally on a windy February morning with the sun shining and the clouds sailing across the sky. I was not in love. I was twenty years old and had been living in Fort Collins for a year. I was engaged to be married and I didn't want to be.

I did not want to hurt him. But I could not marry him. I knew I had to tell him so that night.

He would not be home until evening. I had until then to sit and wait and grieve and dread. The day loomed in front of me, and I knew I could not sit at home, waiting. So, I headed to the barn.

I went to my horse that day, to ride away the afternoon on strong legs built for speed; to tangle my hands in her mane; to lose my pain amidst the thunder of her hooves. We had recently moved Two-Bits to a new barn. This barn was also fifteen minutes from our apartment, tucked into the foothills outside of Fort Collins. The pastures were lined with sturdy wooden fences and the land was surrounded by rolling hills which turned quickly into higher and higher mountains. Trees dotted the property and lined the road leading out of it. My horse waited there among the tall grass for me to come and ride.

She glowed in the mid morning sun, her coat a shiny golden color with a dark dorsal stripe down her back. As I tied her to the hitching post beside the outdoor arena, she danced with anticipation, eager to go. The dancing made me nervous. I was only just becoming strong enough to ride once in a while. And the very power that drew me to Two-Bits was also just a little bit more than my beginner skills could handle.

I brushed her out and cleaned her hooves and tried to make decisions— bareback or a saddle? The ring or the road? And the wind, was there something wrong with the wind?

I couldn't think. I was stuck in the scene I knew would come that evening at home. Bareback or a saddle? The ring or the road? And the wind, was there something wrong with the wind?

I had to go, to move, to get away. I pulled my body on her back and went.

I'd ridden bareback exactly twice before. I'd ridden briefly in the ring two times and planned to try a real ride on real trails sometime soon. Well, now was soon and I had planned all week to go today and try this ride along a gentle trail beside the barn. I had planned and so I went, headed towards that gentle trail, but I changed my mind a moment in. That quiet road was short, and I had five hours to kill.

I chose a different trail, the long one with steep hills and a cliff on one side. I flopped around on my horse's back, clung tight to the reins, and tried not to fall. The truth was, I had no idea how I was expected to hold onto a bareback horse. Do you sit up? Lean forward? Pull your knees up against you like a jockey? Wrap your legs around her belly until your feet almost touch? Hold with your calves? Hold with your thighs? I knew that some of these things would be cues for her to move faster and others would be natural ways for the rider to stay on her back. But I didn't know which was which. I knew nothing about riding bareback, not even enough to realize that her build, so round with barely a withers to hold onto, would challenge even an experienced rider's ability to hold on.

We rode down the longer trail, approaching a hill leading up a straightaway which followed a canyon around a deep mountain lake. The lake was a hundred feet down a sheer drop-off, and we rode along the ridge trail which followed the edge of the cliff. As we headed up the hill, I stabilized, stopped flopping around and got my grip at last. The wind whipped at my face like a wild animal. Dark clouds raced over mountains to my right. To my left, trees danced and bent and fought to keep their hold in the soil. Branches skidded across the path and leaves blew in circles at our feet. When had this storm blown up? I had not noticed. But I had five long hours before this day would end. I couldn't go back now. Instead, I reached for that one place in which fear, and dread were whipped away and only ecstasy remained. I clicked my tongue and knocked my heels against my horse's side. I gave the command for her to run.

She ran. Oh, how she ran. I barely had time to cling to her, to throw myself around her so that I wouldn't fall. Then, all at once, the wind came up and the reins I had been clutching blew out of my hands. One fell to the ground and the other landed across her neck. I held on. She ran faster.

Twice I tried to grab the reins, but they were too far out of reach, and it took all I had to stabilize myself and not fall. One try, two tries, three tries and finally I had the rein across her neck, but only that one. I pulled with all my might. Without slowing, she began to turn.

We were on the trail now, beside the cliff, a hundred-foot drop into a mountain lake, and she was running, no slower than before, off the road, across the grass, and towards that drop. A memory went through my head of someone telling me that horses have no depth perception.

I realized that she could easily plunge us right over that cliff, right off that edge if she believed I was leading her that way, if she trusted my judgment above her shaky depth perception. With only one rein to pull on, I was pointing her right at the edge of that cliff. I was telling her to run over it. With only one rein I could tell her nothing else. I dropped the rein.

She was panicked now, as panicked as I was. All my flopping around on her back confused her, scared her. I was supposed to be in charge. What was going on? She didn't know. And so, she ran. She could run for miles. I could not hold on for miles. At some point, I was going to fall. And when I did, I would not go flying forward or off to the side, but simply slip straight down beneath her feet and be trampled. And if the fall did not kill me, her hooves surely would.

I clung with all I had and knew it would not be enough.

And then I fell.

***

I fell straight down, off my horse's back, losing my grip on her mane and my tenuous hold on her outstretched neck. I fell amidst a thunderous rain of hooves. Hooves—I was aware of hooves as I hit the ground, thundering by me, over me, legs, and speed, missing me and gone.

The instant of the fall split my mind in two. One part remained with my body, reacting in panic, utterly out of control. The other sat apart and watched with perfect rationality, observing, and feeling no pain.

As I fell, the rational voice said, "Good, she missed me with her hooves. She didn't crack my head. I'm still alive."

And as I hit the ground, it said, "My head hit first, before the rest of me. I may have a head injury from that."

It said, "What is all that noise? That screaming?"

It was me. I screamed, not mindless sounds of passion like the movies show, but words of raving like a fool. I'd have been embarrassed to be heard. I screamed as I fell, "No!" and "Oh my God!" and, "God help me! This can't be happening!" When I hit the ground, I screamed, "I'm hurt! Oh God, I'm hurt!" and "Help me! Help me, now!" Somehow, I screamed and screamed, until at last the rational voice in my head ordered me to stop. And I did.

I was lying in the sand on the side of a mountain trail. The trail followed the cliff with the sudden, rocky drop. Normally when I came here, I marveled at the view. Normally I stared out at the mountain peaks, stretching across the skyline. Normally I explored these mountains for hours, at peace with the world. Today there was no peace. Today nothing was normal.

I checked my legs and toes and arms, just like the books from the first aid class I took every year. Wiggle the fingers, wiggle the toes. I could move my neck and look around. Nothing hurt. But something was wrong.

I couldn't move my legs, or my hips, no matter how I tried. And my back—it didn't hurt, but when I moved it, my vision blurred and then went black. I fought to see. I fought to think.

But what was wrong? Nothing hurt. Why was I lying here alone? Was I just a wimp, a coward? Too traumatized to move? Just feeling sorry for myself?

"Get up and walk away!" I shouted at myself out loud. "People fall off horses all the time! Stop being so weak and walk away!" I yelled and yelled but nothing helped. I couldn't will myself to move.

It was then that hysteria truly set in. The rational part of me watched but there was nothing it could do. Everything I thought, my voice hurled into the wind. But I couldn't stop, so I would go on shouting until I forgot that I was doing it and fell silent again. The wind whipped sand against my face and arms so hard it scraped the skin away.

I screamed for help, but the wind was too loud, and my words were lost in it. I found a stick to wave, but there was no one there to see. I was on the edge of a state park trail on the outskirts of Fort Collins. But even the edge was secluded, with no homes or buildings around for as far as I could see. I was half a mile from the trailhead, the road where cars would normally be parked, but there were no cars today. Today there was this storm. It seemed to me to have come up suddenly as I had been riding, but apparently, had I only checked, it had been building long enough for the weather people to put out the word and no one was out on the trails today. No one but me. As time stretched on, I yelled at God.

"God!" I shouted at the top of my lungs, "You have to help me! Send someone to find me, *now*!"

I demanded I be found. When that didn't work, I bargained. I threatened. I swore that I would never believe in God again. I had been struggling with my understanding of God. It was the typical problem. If God was all powerful and could do anything, then how could there be so much suffering in the world? How could a loving God not intervene? Was God, in fact, nothing more than a force of nature, an energy with no consciousness, thoughts or feelings? Was God in fact no different, no more personal, than the wind and the sky? Despite my own personal experience of God as a companion, more and more I was afraid that this companionship was an illusion. That God was just a force of nature, indifferent and removed.

It seemed to me that this was God's chance to prove me wrong. Send help. Show me that I'm not alone. Take care of this crisis and I would know that God was more than the wind in the trees, more than gravity or a roaring river.

And then a man came, finally, fifty feet away, in a yellow tractor. He moved down the trail to a small construction hut set up at the junction of an access road and the main trail. He was above me, and about fifty feet to the left. He got out, went inside the construction trailer, got back into his tractor, and drove away. I yelled at him.

"Don't go! You can't go! You can't leave me here!"

I cried and begged and demanded that he stay, but he never turned his head.

"God!" I shrieked, in rage. "Send someone now or I will never believe in you again!"

Gone was my self-confidence, my strength, my independent soul. Suddenly, all I knew was that I could not be alone. If God existed, someone had to come. God did not exist. So, I gave up.

It was a sudden change. I was entirely at peace.

"All right God." This time I didn't speak out loud. "I disown you. If you exist, I want no part of you. I give you up. I am alone."

I closed my eyes and braced myself, hunkered down and hid my face from wind and sand. I prepared to wait, at peace with that, entirely at peace. An hour passed, then two. But what was time to me? It would be morning before I was found, and I accepted that completely. So completely, in fact, that I barely heard the sound.

It hardly seemed important to open my eyes and look. But a niggling thought forced them open and there I saw a truck coming up the road. Two or three, in fact. But I would be here till tomorrow. I had accepted that. So, I lay my head down quietly to wait.

"A truck." Some part of me tried to make sense of what I'd seen. Those words should have some significance to me.

"Someone's coming who can rescue me." But I'd prepared myself for waiting. What did rescue mean to me?

There was something I should do. As I slipped deeper into silence, some part of me began to scream again. "Someone's coming who can rescue me! Wake up and act! Wake up and act!"

Slowly I opened my eyes. Slowly I lifted my arm to wave. I dropped my arm. The truck drove on.

I closed my eyes and dropped my head. I was resigned to waiting but still a voice inside me screamed. "No! You have to stop the truck!"

The truck. Oh, yes, the truck. I lifted my head. I lifted my arm. One more effort I'd grudgingly make before I'd close my eyes again. I did not expect the truck to stop. I did not think that it was really there.

The trucks stopped, not far away. Tires, doors and legs, a man, running towards me. I was no longer alone.

The man knelt and talked. The rest of his crew gathered around. I told him of my horse. "My horse, where is my horse? She may be hurt. My horse…"

He knew first aid and asked my name. He checked me over—wiggle the fingers, wiggle the toes. I tried to tell him what I already knew: my right hip and my lower back. But he didn't hear my words. When he was done, he assured me I would be all right. He would call an ambulance. My right hip, he told me, and my lower back.

They covered me with their coats to protect me from the wind, to stop the sand that cut my arms. They knelt by my side to keep the coats from blowing off and tucked them around my face and head. I didn't know how many men. I didn't know how many trucks. In the darkness, I drifted in and out and knew that I was safe. Whatever happened, I was not alone.

The ambulance came and they moved me with a sheet. I screamed, "Oh, God! Oh, God! Oh, God!" through gritted teeth and pain. Then I lay still again.

They drove slowly so as not to jostle me. No sirens and no flashing lights. They stopped outside a hospital in town.

***

As I lay in the hospital emergency room with doctors and nurses rushing all around, a doctor pulled back the blue curtain around my bed and bustled in. He pinned the x-rays to a lightboard on the right of my bed. My back was broken. My pelvis too. It was possible I would never walk again. Only time would tell.

I looked up. Across the room the door to the ER opened and there stood Andy, still for a moment, getting his bearings. I saw him as through a tunnel, suddenly just him and me, and my stomach clenched. I was going to leave him. I *wanted* to leave him. I was angry and frustrated after months of trying to fit myself into a life I no longer wanted, of trying to deny important parts of myself. Then a part of me began to speak. Calmly and rationally, it spoke. "You are hurt, possibly seriously. You can't do this now. This has to go away."

And it did. I watched as that calm voice took from inside me all of my feelings, my anger and frustration, my desire to be free, my very unhappiness, and stuffed it carefully into a box. I watched as that part of me closed the box and sealed it well, then shoved that box so far inside of myself I no longer knew that it was there. And as Andy caught sight of me and rushed to my side, I sighed in relief to see him, wanting nothing more than to settle into his arms. I forgot. I forgot about my unhappiness and my plans to leave. I forgot it all. It was months before I was well enough to begin to feel the discontent again. It was over a year before I even remembered that I had been planning on leaving him that day.

I cannot excuse my use of him except to say that I did not do it on purpose. I did not intend to take advantage of him. It was survival, instinct. It was my subconscious mind taking over to save my life. And somewhat, it was cowardice as well. It had taken everything I had inside me to gather the courage I would need to tell him I did not want to marry him. Hurt and overwhelmed, I simply didn't have it in me to follow through on that now.

* * *

I spent a week in the hospital, learning to walk again. I was in a full body brace, unable to move or even turn over on my own. The first night, after Andy had gone home, I lay in my hospital room unable to sleep, tears sliding down my cheeks, and wondered if the hospital had a chaplain on duty. Was there someone who could come, to pray with me, to read from the bible or just to hold my hand? I wanted a Catholic priest, though I was as Protestant as they come. I wanted my dad.

My dad had known from the start that he didn't want to raise us Catholic. He saw too many problems with the Catholic church. But he was Catholic through and through. When my mom became a minister, he made a point of

47

going to her church with the family every Sunday, but on Saturdays he went to mass.

My father loved to learn. By the end of his life, he had a PhD and four master's degrees. We would sit together on long car drives or in the lazy boys in his living room and talk about philosophy or religion, what I believed and how I experienced the world. He shared his journeys some too but most of all he listened to mine. He offered guidance as well and shared his beliefs. But most of all he wanted to know what I thought, what I experienced and who I was turning out to be. He found my words exciting. He rejoiced in me.

When I was young, I didn't understand my dad. I thought he should be a male version of my mother and did not see the value of what he was instead.

I did not hide from him my disappointment and my pain. I let him know he'd failed me, sent him long essays about how he'd let me down: He wasn't home enough, he wasn't involved enough in the family, he didn't show his love the way I thought he should. I listed all the ways he'd failed me.

***

Andy called my family the evening of my accident and told everyone what was going on. We all agreed that it was not reasonable for anyone to come out right away. I lived a 15-hour drive away from my father and further than that from my mother, and last-minute plane tickets would be exorbitant. The doctors said I would be in the hospital at least a week, and that when I went home, I would need help. Lots of help. My mother, with difficulty, agreed to wait until I was out of the hospital, and she could come help me out at home. My father agreed the same.

He couldn't do it. While I lay there that night wanting my dad, he got on a late-night plane and came to me. He couldn't stay away. There was nothing he could do—it was ridiculous for him to come. I would need him much more later and there was no way he could afford two tickets or so much time away from work. Logically, he should have waited. But he couldn't stay away.

He was there the next morning when I woke, sitting in a chair in the corner of my room, looking lost. When I opened my eyes, he stood up, took a tentative step forward and stretched out his hand. The nurse rushed past him, and he sat back down. There was nothing for him to do.

So, he sat. He sat that whole week while I learned to walk again, sometimes screaming, and passing out from the pain. He sat with his ashen face in the corner unable to help. And he gave me all I ever needed from him again.

I saw something in his face that week, as he watched me struggle, something that I never doubted again. I saw love. Pure, undiluted love. He may not always have known exactly what I wanted him to say. He may have had trouble knowing what to do. But any deficiency in those areas was not for lack of love. His love was complete, perhaps the most solid thing about him. And I saw too that when I truly needed him, he would always be there. At the end of the week, when he went home, my relationship with him was healed.

***

For a month, I lay in bed in a full body brace, needing help even to turn over. Andy's parents came, and my mom, taking turns and staying for weeks at a time. As for me, something had happened during that accident. Something that affected every part of me. My body had broken, yes. But somehow something else had broken too. I couldn't say what. I felt it snap in the initial striking of the ground when I fell and ever since, something deep inside me was still. It left me quiet inside, as though it was not only my body that had to stay still to heal, but my soul as well.

I healed. First the brace, then a wheelchair. Eventually a cane. By then it had been months, and I was again feeling my discontent with Andy. Some part of me, a petty part, felt that this accident had worked out well for Andy. I was again helpless and needing him. I stopped demanding more of him emotionally than he wanted to give. But as I healed it all returned: my need

49

for more. Andy and I simply wanted different things out of life. Eventually it had to end.

Chapter 6

A Horse Of My Own

During my time in Fort Collins, I had come across a book called *The Celestine Prophesy*. I don't remember much about the book now, but what I do remember—what I have always remembered—was the idea that the earth is a vast library and the answers to all the questions in the universe are encoded in the DNA of everything around us. I became convinced in some spiritual, not-quite-literal-sense that if I could just connect to nature, I could find the answers I needed to be healthy again. I could heal. This started me on a sacred relationship with nature. I saw God in nature. I saw God as nature. I saw every living and non-living thing as Holy. And I knew, I *knew*, that if I could only understand them, they would set me free.

* * *

I was newly out of a wheelchair and walking with a cane. I had broken up with Andy and was going to Michigan to live with my mother.

I arrived in Michigan with boxes full of dried herbs, old bottles and beeswax, tinctures, and teas, and I set up my own apothecary in a bedroom upstairs in my mother's house. I was considering going back to school. There was a small college which was well respected in Kalamazoo, just up the street from where my mother lived. I wanted to study medicine and plants and become a Naturopathic Physician. But the fatigue had started to return along with my accident, and the arthritis as well, and I was once again struggling to balance what I wanted to do with a body that couldn't keep up.

For a couple months, my mother helped me rest, building up my strength for school and finally healing from my long ordeal. Around then, we started to hear about a healer in Michigan who had great success with autoimmune diseases. He treated his patients using only whole foods and when he saw me, he started out by prescribing three months of eating twelve tangerines and two cups of Collard Greens every other day. I'd never had Collard Greens before, but I found I craved the food he prescribed. For a year, I followed his prescriptions, one food after another. Nothing was changing and everyone thought I was nuts. But his approach spoke to me in a way that other medical approaches did not. I stuck with it, barely, and finished out the year. And on the last day of his year-long plan, the arthritis I had struggled with all that time went away.

It was gone. No more pain in my joints. No more swelling. Overnight, it went away. I can't say if it was his treatment that did it or if it was just a coincidence of timing. JRA often goes away when the sufferer is in their early twenties. So maybe it would have happened anyway. Whatever the reason, I was overjoyed, but also now found myself in a difficult situation. The fatigue remained and soon it became more intense than ever.

My doctors had long been waffling between the two diagnoses: JRA and Lupus and with the removal of the arthritis, both of these diagnoses were now being questioned. Now, instead of the support of doctors, I was told, "There is nothing wrong with you," and sent on my way.

But there *was* something wrong. At times, the fatigue became so bad that I couldn't walk around the block. But fatigue is illusive and hard to quantify. And at other times I could go hiking, camping, do all the things that I loved. Yes, those things came with a deep inner fatigue that never quite went away, but that was easy enough to push aside when I was rested. I could push through, doing what I wanted to do despite the ache in my chest, the creeping pain in my muscles. Then I had times when I could barely lift my head off the pillow, so I would rest for a week or a month or—yes, sometimes a year— until my old energy would come back. Maybe not all of it. But most of it anyway. It was hard for doctors to quantify and harder for them to understand, this up and down pendulum that was my life. And so most simply didn't believe.

I had become so passionate about healing, about finding a way for the body to thrive, that I wanted to get on with spending my life helping others do that too. Never mind that I had not yet found a way to help myself. I wanted to study pre-med and hoped to go to one of the four Naturopathic Medical schools that then existed in the United States. My mother and her partner had agreed to help me get through school, though I would be living in the dorms once classes started. They'd drive me to doctor's appointments and do my laundry, clean my room, and generally help with anything that would allow me the time to study and to rest. I jumped in with both feet, forgetting, as I always did, what this body told me every day: *slow down*. I didn't slow down. I loved school. I had always loved school and being back on campus, back in classrooms, was exciting. I loved living in the dorms. Never mind that I was a good bit older than the other students now. I was back doing what I wanted to do, on the way to the life I dreamed of.

So here I was, recovered enough to begin taking classes again. And my search for an explanation for the problems of my body hit a wall. The fatigue couldn't be objectively measured by outsiders, and I began to be told that I was fine, that I had clearly had JRA, and it had cleared up. That there was nothing wrong with me anymore.

Get a hobby.

You're just depressed.

You're twenty-two and you live in your mother's house, that's the problem.

* * *

I was in my second year at Kalamazoo College. I was an Resident Assistant (RA) in my new school and loved my blue room in the top story of an old brick house on campus. The residents took turns cooking dinner together and argued over the ethics of the practice the college had of hiring someone to come in and clean for us once a week. Is it inherently demeaning, some of them asked, to be asked to clean up after another person? I pointed out that with my illness I could not manage college if someone didn't clean up after me, not to mention making my food and doing my laundry. Maybe, I suggested, it was only demeaning if you saw that work as beneath the dignity of a regular person. Maybe the problem wasn't in accepting help but in appreciating it adequately.

I loved my classes but struggled every day. I was walking normally now, my pelvis and back having mostly healed, but my exhaustion was high, and I was in pain most of the time, not from arthritis now, but from the effects of the fatigue. Some days I was too weak to go to class and on those days, my mom's partner would go for me, taking notes and tape recording the lecture. Sue was only working part time and she brought my laundry back and forth, putting it away for me when it was done. She also brought me meals when I was too tired to manage the dining room, carefully made to my mother's specifications with a pretty place mat and a cloth napkin *("She needs beauty to heal as much as she needs food," my mom would say.)*

But in the midst of all of this, my heart ached constantly. It ached for Two-Bits. Despite everything, I had come to love that horse more deeply than I'd ever thought possible. I thought about her every day. Having a horse was ridiculous at this time in my life. I was barely managing to keep up with my classes. Where would I keep her? When would I see her? And how could I afford her? But I couldn't let her go. I held nothing about the accident against her. I knew it had been my fault, my decisions that put us at that time in that place. I also knew by now that she was way too much horse for me, but I believed (erroneously) that I would someday grow into her. And I missed everything about her. Without her there was a hole in my life. Not having her there felt like I was missing a piece of my soul.

I had no job and no money. I had no ability to get one. I could never afford to buy her, even if the camp would sell her to me. And then I could.

* * *

My mom came over to my room on the second story of the old brick house on the edge of campus. It was a spring day and the trees outside my window were covered in bright white buds. She had a gift for me, she said. Sitting on the edge of my small, twin bed, she told me that her mother, who had died when I was two, had left some investments to her and her sister. Not much, but they got a little every year—a few thousand dollars apiece. This year they had cashed in on one of those investments and wanted to give the money it brought equally to each of their mother's grandkids. The five of us would get $1500 each. And she handed me a check.

I sat on my bed long after she had left thinking, my heart racing. Finally, I picked up the phone.

"Hi! It's Christie," I said, "I'm calling about Two-Bits."

"Oh," Nancy said, "Let me put Ken on. He deals with the horses more than I do."

"I've been thinking a lot about Two-Bits," I told him, "And I miss that horse something awful. I think about her all the time. I just wanted to say that if you ever decide to sell her, I would like you to let me know."

"Well, funny you should say that" Ken replied, "We just made up a list of horses to sell this year and she is on it."

"How much?" I asked, holding my breath.

"$1500," he said, and she was mine.

* * *

I worked at camp again that summer, doing whatever jobs I had the energy to do and earning the money it would take to ship Two-Bits to

55

Michigan when the season was over. It was early September when I stood in the gravel driveway of a small farmhouse outside of Kalamazoo, under a large walnut tree. Behind me a ten-acre pasture stretched out like heaven, with grass that was chest high and sturdy wooden fences. There was a traditional looking barn with two stalls to my right. The house sat on a quiet dirt street across the street from my doctor's house. I had found the place through him, and his teenage daughter was going to help me care for Two-Bits. My mom and Sue had agreed to drive me out there twice a day to do her feeding and they stood with me in the driveway, waiting eagerly. It was 2 am in the morning.

Down the street the lumbering lights of a big rig turned ponderously onto the little dirt road. The truck drew up in front of us and stopped with a sigh and a hiss. Two men swung out of the cab and came around to shake our hands. "She did just fine," they assured me. "All ready to go."

They attached a steep ramp and slid open a large door on the side of the trailer. Inside were stalls to the right and the left with horses in them. I had eyes for only one horse. She walked off calmly, like she owned the place.

It was dark and we were trying not to wake the inhabitants of the little farmhouse who had agreed to rent us this pasture. I led Two-Bits away from the truck while Sue tipped the drivers for me and thanked them. The big truck lumbered on its way down the quiet street. I took Two-Bits to her new pasture, talking quietly to her all the time.

"You are mine now and I will always take care of you. This is your new home. I think you will like it. I'll be out every day to see you. Everything is going to be all right."

I walked her around the pasture in the dark, letting her see the boundaries and sniff the water trough. Then I broke off a flake of hay and tucked it into her feeder for the night. Not that she needed it. She had all the grass she could eat in that pasture already. I stood with her until I finally couldn't ignore that my mother, who had come out to help and be part of the excitement, needed to get home to bed. She had work tomorrow. Sue agreed to bring me out to see Two-Bits in the morning after we'd gotten some rest.

* * *

For the first year Two-Bits lived amongst the tall grass next to the quiet farmhouse outside of town. For a year, I had brought my homework to her field, sitting with her while she grazed, rarely up for riding, but spending hours doing massage and grooming and just talking to her. She watched for me to come and stood near me when I was there. She had always been a horse who reveled in being a horse—physical and beautiful and full of power. She looked down on the weak and the weary. The thing was, I may have been weak in body, but I wasn't weak in my mind. And to a horse it is the mental, the emotional strength that matters most. And so, she respected me. She loved me. But slowly, as my year in Michigan moved on, my abilities in this regard began to fail.

My illness began to affect not only my body, but also my mind. For the first time, I had trouble thinking clearly. I would start a sentence and not be able to finish it. I, who loved to spend hours debating politics and religion, could hardly form a coherent thought some days. And with that my inner strength, my will, my emotional core, began to fail. On those days, the days when I was dazed and confused and she could push me around, Two-Bits seemed disappointed in me. Like I had failed her in some way.

And so, over time as I worsened, we moved Two-Bits to a facility that could take care of her when I was not around. And I was around less and less, increasingly unable to make the drive across town to her new stables: Increasingly unable to do anything but try desperately to get my work done for class and then fall, exhausted, into bed.

* * *

That first December, just after I finished school, I got a call from a friend. He was flying to Chicago to spend a week with his childhood buddies.

One of them had an apartment on The Loop and had invited everyone over to spend New Year's week bumming around Chicago and taking in the sights. He knew I had been sick for a while and needed some cheering up. Did I want to come along? The train from Kalamazoo to Chicago was an easy ride, only 3 hours.

I was a year out of my relationship with Andy, but only just starting to think of dating anyone else. Mike was one of my closest friends. Maybe friends of his would be good people. In any case, I was eager to do something fun in the big city and Mike said they would look out for me when my energy got bad, so I took the train to Chicago. Mike and his friend, Dave, picked me up from the train station. Dave had a nice car, a condo in downtown Chicago and a 9-5 job. He wore slacks and a polo, having just come from work. I immediately dismissed him as a potential romantic possibility. He looked too grown up. I dated college kids or cowboys. He was nothing like the kind of partner I pictured at that point in my life.

That week I slept on Dave's living room floor with the rest of the guys from his neighborhood, ate dinner at Navy Pier and went to dance clubs in the evenings. When my energy didn't last as long as everyone else's, Dave took to walking me home early so I could go to bed. We talked about life, and I held onto his arm as he escorted me to his condo each evening. Slowly I began to change my opinion of him. Dave was kind and quiet, strong, and funny. One morning I heard Dave talking to Mike in the kitchen. "So, what's the story with Christie? What is her illness? How sick is she and is there any chance she will ever recover?" They talked about me for a while as I pretended to still be asleep. Dave pondered what he learned. At the end of the week, as he prepared to drive me to the train station, I asked him if he would consider making the three-hour trip to go out to dinner with me sometime. He said yes, and, wanting to be sure there was no misunderstanding, I said, "You know I mean on a date, right?"

"Yes," he assured me, "I got that."

Dave and I began dating. Either he would make the three-hour trip to Kalamazoo, or I would take the train to see him in Chicago. Those visits were magical. Dave had a good job and no responsibilities to speak of. We went out to dinner when we wanted to, went to shows and hung out at the neighborhood bar where he was friends with the bar tender and knew the local crowd. Then I would sleep all day while he was at work, and he would come home to me in the evening. Dave loved to cook and would make me good meals on nights when we decided to stay in. He understood my low energy and was always ready with an arm or a hand, always willing to change plans at the last minute. He seemed to enjoy introducing me to his friends. We dated for a number of months and our time together was magical. He had no more interest in hiking or riding horses than Andy did, but he celebrated my love of these things. He did everything he could to enable me to do the things I loved whether they involved him or not.

* * *

My life was a constant fight with pain and exhaustion. I pushed every minute to try and keep up with my classes. It was fall in Michigan and I drove every week to my doctor's office for acupuncture and other treatments. And every drive took me down this one road, an old state highway lined with trees that turned brilliant purples, reds, and oranges in their fall display. And during the fall, when the leaves were at their height, every time I would drive this road I would cry. I would sob. I would wail like my heart was broken. And I didn't know why.

Finally, one day I cried so hard I had to pull over. And as I sat there, my head resting on the steering wheel, I finally thought to ask, *why?* Why did I cry every time I drove this road? It was the most beautiful road I'd ever driven with the brilliant colors of fall showing off for all they were worth. And yet, my tears were not for beauty. They were tears of sorrow. Of heartbreak. Of pain. I sat in my car, surrounded by nature's most spectacular show and asked myself, for the first time, why it hurt so much to see? And the answer came to me at last.

I cried because I couldn't stop and appreciate it. I had to get to my doctor's appointment then home to do homework and rest, rest, rest, as fast as I could. I cried because I couldn't stop and enjoy one of the most beautiful spectacles on earth. I cried because I was missing it. Because I was missing everything I loved as I tried with all my might to make it through school. And that was that.

I knew I would not be returning to school for the next semester. It was time to find a life which would allow me to live at peace with this illness, a life in which I wouldn't be missing out on the things that I loved the most. At the end of the fall semester I left school, returning to my mother's house and my bottles of herbs that lined the walls. I rested for six months until summer came, then moved Two-Bits across the country to work at camp again for the summer.

I had known from the start that Dave and I weren't permanent. For one thing, I had returned to not being interested in marriage. But more than that, I was pretty sure that in the long run I needed someone more like me— someone who wanted to live in in the mountains and hike in the wilderness. I couldn't imagine that a computer programmer who had never been camping in his life would ever really work for me. Yes, I loved being with him. He made me feel cared for and safe. We went out to nice restaurants and did the big city thing. But the big city thing was vacation for me, not everyday life. It was something I waned in short spurts, not the kind of life I wanted to live permanently. So, when the time came for me to return to camp, I broke up with Dave. He took it stoically, letting me know that he didn't agree with my decision to break up but accepting that it was something I had to do.

CHAPTER 7

Mice and Lions

The summer camp where I'd met Andy, the one that had owned Two-Bits, had become an important staple in my life. This had become a home for me, a healing place in the mountains where I mattered, regardless of what my body could or could not do. Each summer, they set me up in a cabin and had me do odd jobs, running programs and helping out where I could. I didn't have the energy to be a counselor. I couldn't keep up with the kids all day. But I did other things and made a difference, and I loved it.

I slept most afternoons. Even though I didn't have campers of my own, the summers was exhausting, grueling, but also meaningful. I started to think about what kind of life I could build for myself, given my illness. I knew that medical school was beyond me. I had long ago let go of law school. I mourned the loss of both of them. I mourned the loss of my dreams. I knew there must be a life out there I was meant to live, something wonderful and better than all that I was giving up. But I didn't know what it was.

As the summer drew to a close, I decided that I wanted to live in Colorado, somewhere remote where I could be in touch with the wildness and the wild world. And I had an idea that if I pushed myself to live somewhere remote, somewhere dangerous, where I *had* to be physically fit to survive, my will would finally triumph, and I would conquer this illness which had so long dragged me down. I would have to. Mind over matter; I was sure this was the answer.

At this time in my life, I was an odd mix of elated at the very process of living and dragged down by the barriers of my body. I saw the natural world as almost Holy, and I craved to live closer to it. I had little interest in church but felt God's presence in my daily life.

I was studying Christian Science. There are a lot of misunderstandings out there about Christian Science. While the religious traditions of Christian Science were a bit conservative for me, I was astounded by the core of the teachings. This religion was an attempt to reclaim the original physical healing which had been such a central part of Christ's teachings and Christianity's first purpose. The founder of Christian Science had lived much like me; with an illness no-one could define plaguing her adult life. Then one day she was in a buggy accident and lay on her death bed, too injured to survive. She had picked up The Bible and begun to read and came to understand something in the words that went beyond what most of us see. And she was healed. She claimed this healing was available to anyone if only they would see what she had seen—the Truth of existence, the Reality of our Spirit, and the Unreality of our bodies. I had seen it work for others, heard of people with miraculous healings. I was trying to claim this for myself.

It was also my belief that we are all created with a purpose and that our best lives lie in following that purpose. I wanted to find my purpose. I offered myself to God—*whatever you need from me, I will give. You take care of the details, the how and the what and I will go where you lead.*

I knew that whatever my purpose was, whatever God wanted me to do, would make my heart sing. I was looking for a life I could love every bit as much as the ones I had dreamed of before.

✳ ✳ ✳

One afternoon towards the end of the summer, I borrowed a friend's car and went driving out north towards Estes Park, into the high mountains near Rocky Mountain National Park. I had heard of a cabin for rent, $400 per month, far up a mountain. It was off-grid, with no electricity or running water, and I felt pulled to it, called to it. I was thinking of moving there and was off to see it for the first time.

Before I left, I rifled through my duffel bag, looking for a cassette tape to play on my drive. To my surprise I came up with one I had gotten from one of my parents, I don't remember which. It was religious music by the St. Louis Jesuits, a tape I had loved when I was younger and lost many years ago. I had been raised in a house that honored religion, though criticized it too. As such I had developed a deep love of how religion spoke to my life as well as a harsh criticism of the harm it so often caused in the world. But the music, I loved the music.

I hadn't seen this cassette tape in years and don't know how it ended up in my bag that day. But I put it on and listened to the music wash over me. *"Here I am, Lord. Is it I, Lord? I have heard you calling in the night. I will go, Lord. If you need me. I will hold your people in my heart."*

I drove up the narrow, winding highway through Thompson Canyon until I reached the tiny town of Drake, Colorado. Just a couple of buildings and a church. I pulled over to see what this little town might have to offer. It was the nearest town to the cabin I was looking at. If I moved here, this would be my home.

I walked to the church. It was a small, one-room, white church with a steeple, and on the sign board out front were the words, *"Here I am, Lord. I will go, Lord."*

This was the place. I drove up the long, winding, one-lane road cut into the side of a cliff and saw the cabin. Sitting in a meadow at the top of this mountain, it couldn't have been more perfect. My heart sang.

* * *

I moved into my cabin, an A-frame with a weathered wooden porch surrounding it on three sides. One wall I lined with jars of bulk flours, grains, pasta and various kinds of dehydrated fruits and vegetables. Gutters caught rainwater off the roof and funneled it into a holding tank where it stayed until I boiled it for drinking or to shower or wash the dishes. Above the water tank, I hung an old-fashioned washboard which I used to scrub my clothes.

I lived for many months in this cabin, far from roads, with no electricity or running water and only my horse for transportation. I caught rainwater off the roof, walked through snow to get to the outhouse and heated my one-room-cabin with wood which I split with an ax. My cabin was at an elevation of 7000 feet, a harsh world of evergreens and aspen trees, early snow and cold nights.

Amidst a vast blanket of wildflowers and surrounded by towering, snow-covered peaks, I strung fences to make a pasture and built a barn with a hammer and a hand saw. I built a home for Two-Bits, and we moved in together. In the fall, I watched as a herd of elk, stretching as far as the eye could see, moved across the pasture, mingled with my horse, and raised their heads to notice me. Occasionally, wild horses would come and call to my mare. Once she left with them and I spent three long days tracking the herd before I was able to bring her back.

I spent mornings wandering the forests on horseback, and when food got short, I rode hard all day, making my way down the mountain to tie my horse outside the local post office across from the church and buy groceries at the small country store.

I made friends with the mountain men who lived in teepees further up the hill. I baked bread for them, and they dragged old trees to my front door for me to use as firewood. They taught me to harvest rose hips for extra vitamin C in the winter and how to find the hidden stashes of food, sometimes money and survival gear that mountain folks keep deep within the national forests for emergencies. Each had their own stash, hidden somewhere, and I learned the secrets of many of them. I was with a friend one day when he went to check on his stash and found that a bear had beaten him to it. Cans of food and bags of beans were scattered all over the clearing with hundred-dollar bills floating around, stuck in bushes and the high branches of trees.

I spent countless evenings sitting around campfires listening to stories or just being silent in the company of men who dressed in animal furs and hunted antlers for a living.

I loved this life. I lived for the romance of it. I loved the reality of it. But the reality could be harsh. Sometimes it tested even my love.

There are mice in mountain cabins—sometimes hundreds of them. I would wake up at night to find them under my blankets or running across my face. They would knock jars off of counters and walk brazenly across my table as I ate breakfast. I did everything I could to try and discourage them, but they overran my efforts at every turn.

Summer in the mountains is brief. By September I had snow, and it would last well into June. Every morning, I would wake up under mounds of heavy blankets to find that the temperature in my cabin was below freezing. I would have to dress in the frigid air, before beginning, with stiff, frozen fingers, the time-consuming process of starting a fire in my wood stove. I would have to dress in multiple layers of heavy clothes and coats, cumbersome hats, huge bulky gloves and clunky snow boots every time I wanted to go to the outhouse, and then I would have to shovel open the door, remove the many layers of clothes and sit half naked in temperatures as low as twenty below.

If I were sick with the flu or anything else, I still needed to split my wood, start my fire, and cook my food over an open flame. I would still have to walk to the pasture in three feet of snow to feed my horse and, if her water system had frozen, spend all day hauling buckets of water from the nearest pond.

I never got anything but a cold shower. By the end of the winter I would sweat all day, shoveling snow and splitting wood, be covered with hay from feeding my horse, dirt from traveling on the mountain paths and smoke from sitting by fires, and I would stay that way for weeks before I cared enough to wash in that bitter cold.

I began to see lion tracks on the path to the outhouse. Between the cold and the mountain lions, I soon decided that peeing in a can at night was not such a bad idea. My friends on the mountain would tell me that the bear were getting bold and coming right into their teepees while they slept.

I buried pets which were my only companions, my family, but didn't make it through the harshness of mountain living. I began to find that the novelty of four hours of hard riding any time I ran out of milk was slowly wearing off, and never being able to get the eggs home from the grocery store unbroken was no longer quite so quaint. I knew the deep, cold panic of waking up to a raging blizzard the morning after I let myself run out of firewood.

There was no 911, no police and no fire trucks, no ambulance to reach me if I had need of them.

And those mountain men I had befriended? They stockpiled guns, carried knives, and began drinking beer at breakfast. They had parties at which best friends attacked each other with knives because they got too drunk to realize that small annoyances weren't worth killing over. When they left the mountain, they would stop on the road to pick up roadkill to keep until they reached home and could prepare it as food or claim its hide to use as clothing.

Anyone who lives this life soon discovers that it is not only romance. It is also unending hard work, constant discomfort and sometimes tragedy. It is beautiful. It is also crude and cruel and dangerous. But my body thrived. My energy built up again, coming back to me so that I felt almost normal most days, as long as I slept for a few hours every afternoon. I hiked and rode my horse and spent time with my neighbors and I had never loved life more.

***

Me and Two-Bits against the world. I rode her more at my remote cabin than I had anywhere else, mostly out of necessity. I was surrounded all day by the beauty of nature, and I could sit until evening on the porch of my cabin, watching the elk roam and the breezes blow. This was beauty I would not miss out on because I was too busy, too rushed to take it in.

During this time, my mother sent me a few hundred dollars a month, everything she could spare from a minister's salary. And my older brother began to do the same. One day he came to visit, and he had with him a three-ring binder labeled, "Share the wealth." My brother has an amazing head for math and at this time he was earning much of his income by gambling. He could gamble all day without getting caught up in the emotions of the wins and losses and he won slow, steady money that really added up. He promised me 20% of everything he earned gambling and from then on, I would receive a check from him periodically with enough money to keep me going for a while longer. And so, I lived on the generosity of others. I also kept in touch with Dave. We had started talking again shortly after I moved. We talked about him flying me out to visit sometime after the summer passed. But I couldn't leave my horse so that would have to wait.

***

One morning I awoke to temperatures in their twenties. Not as bad as some days, but cold, cold, cold. I pulled the mounds of covers over my head, refusing for a moment to consider crawling out of the warm bed into that frigid air. But Two-Bits was waiting, and her breakfast was all that would keep her warm through this cold day. So finally, I heaved the covers back and leapt out of bed. Not even bothering to change my underwear or take off my nightshirt, I pulled on long johns, then leggings, then jeans. Then I pulled two sweatshirts over my head, put on a warm hat, and shoved my feet into my boots. I stumbled down the ladder to the main part of the cabin and with frigid fingers began trying to light a fire. I shivered as I set up the kindling, my numb fingers fumbling with the match, then crumpled up a piece of newspaper and stuffed it under the little pile I had gathered. I struggled to light the match and get my fire going for the day. Once I had it roaring, I banked it back, pulled on my gloves, and stumbled outside.

67

The day was clear and blue with the sun already high in the sky. I headed towards the pasture to feed my horse. The first indication that something was wrong was the broken wire next to her gate. I looked around in alarm and finally spotted Two-Bits in the far end of the pasture. I could see the blood from there.

Two-Bits had two large gashes across her chest, with myriad additional cuts here and there. She had barbed wire stuck to the gashes and tangled around her legs. She was heaving, breathing heavily in and out, her eyes wide and her nostrils flared. Just the sight of her sent me into a panic. But I didn't have the luxury of panic. I was her only help.

I talked soothingly to her as I quietly approached. I ran my hand carefully over her neck, asking her to stay still. And I evaluated her plight. It would take wire cutters to get the wire loose safely. She would need stitches. I told her to stay, implored her to stay where she was and not to move. And I ran to the house for my wire cutters.

I was back as quickly as I could. I had set a tea-pot full of ice on the stove in the cabin to melt. At these temperatures, my water always froze overnight. So, I put the kettle, now full of ice from my water the day before, on the woodstove to heat. I hoped to have water soon to wash her wounds.

When I returned to the pasture, I knelt carefully in front of her and began the long, arduous process of removing the wire from her chest and legs. Her legs were relatively free of the deep gashes which populated her chest. But barbed wire is evil stuff, and it can cause as much damage coming off as going on. It took me an hour to slowly unravel it, unsticking the barbs from her skin and setting the cut off pieces of wire aside. When, finally, I had it done, I put the halter on her and carefully, painstakingly, walked her back to the house where I had a hitching post to tie her to. I went inside to find the water melted in the kettle I had put on the wood stove an hour before. I brought it out with fresh cotton squares and slowly, carefully began cleaning up her cuts. As each long gash was cleaned, and I wiped the tears out of my own eyes again and again, I smeared wound cream on her cuts, knowing it wasn't enough. Finally, I got her some hay, and, leaving her tied to the hitching post, I set out for the nearest neighbor's house. I walked three miles to find a neighbor with a car and I begged them to drive me into town.

They agreed. They drove me to a pay phone at the bottom of the mountain and I called the nearest vet. "No," the vet said. There was no way he could come all the way up there to treat my horse. I called another vet and another. Finally, one of them spoke frankly to me. "No one is going to make it up there this time of year. Most of us don't have trucks that could make it up that mountain with the road the way it is. You are going to have to treat her yourself." And he agreed to bring me the supplies I would need to do so. My neighbor waited patiently in the nearby bar (I had bought him lunch and a beer for his trouble). The vet drove to the bar and met me in the parking lot. A young man with short cropped hair and a warm winter coat, he handed me a bag of supplies. Then he took each out one at a time and walked me through what I would have to do.

I arrived back at my cabin three hours after leaving to find Two-Bits quietly resting by the hitching post. I hadn't known if she would be there. She had a bad habit of pulling back when tied to anything she didn't like and could easily have broken her rope and run away. But I imagined her wounds hurt and I think she trusted me. She knew that I would return and make it all okay.

I spent the rest of the afternoon carefully cleaning each wound. The worst two would have to be stitched. I used a tiny needle to numb up the surrounding tissue with lidocaine, as I had been instructed. Then, using a rounded needle with thread attached, I carefully began mimicking the stitches the vet had shown me. I pulled out the old cloth he had used to show me the pattern and copied it as best I could.

In the meantime, some of the other neighbors had heard about my horse and come down to fix the broken fence for me. As they finished up, they gathered around my horse. "You need to know," One of them said, his hat in his hand, as he ran his hand through his damp hair, "There are lion tracks in that pasture. It was a lion that ran her through that fence for sure."

A lion. And it might come back. "I'm sleeping in the pasture tonight," I declared. They looked at me skeptically.

"And what will you do if it returns? Do you even own a gun?"

Well, no. I didn't own a gun.

"Do you have gear for sleeping in that kind of cold? It got down to twenty degrees last night."

I knew that. I thought I could bring my sleeping gear from the house out to the pasture and sleep in the three-sided barn I had built for Two-Bits when we had first moved in. Protection from the wind, but I would be right there to protect her if danger came. Not that I knew what I could do, myself alone against a lion. But I would do something. She would not be alone.

The men muttered and grumbled but they were not accustomed to telling others what they could or could not do. Finally, one of them loaned me a gun, two or three came back with sleeping bags rated for winter weather and they got me settled to their satisfaction. "Be careful," they told me, "Lions are nothing to mess with."

Three nights I slept in that barn, staying with my horse, but no lion ever came back. Eventually I returned the borrowed gear and moved back inside.

***

This particular month, money was tight. Two-Bits had needed care and I had spent most of what should have been my rent money on that. The day came for rent to be due and I didn't have it. I didn't have any of it. I was in a panic.

I paced all morning, trying to come up with a plan. I was angry. Hadn't I made a deal with God that I would go where he sent me, but he had to take care of the details? He had to tell me how to pay the rent? Wasn't that my deal? And now what, I had no rent, and my landlord would come by in just four hours and what would I tell him? I paced. I ranted. *What about our deal, God?*

And then I stopped. What *about* our deal? I had agreed to do whatever God called me to do and God would take care of the details. The rent. The food. The heat. So, what was I so worried about? Paying the rent wasn't my job. Why was I taking it on as though it were?

I sat down and took a breath. "Okay, God. This is our deal. This is still our deal. I'll trust you. It's up to you." And I went about my day.

An hour later I heard a knock on the door. Curry was running down to town to get his mail. Did I want to come with him? Yes. I did. We lumbered down the mountain in Curry's old black truck, alternately chatting and sitting in silence. We got the mail.

In the mail that day I got a letter from a couple I had not heard from since I was a teenager, living in Winthrop, Iowa. They had heard about the adventure I was having, living out here on this mountain, and they wanted to help. They enclosed a check for $400 to help cover whatever I needed. I closed my eyes, a lump in my throat. *How was it that I deserved any part of this marvelous life?*

***

Later that winter, I came back from dinner around the campfire with a friend to find my cabin ablaze with fire. We saw it from a way off and I shouted for my friend to stop. I jumped from the car and began to run, my friend throwing open the gate behind me and rushing to my side. The cabin was bursting with fire and there was little we could do.

My landlord was home this night and while my friend pounded on his door, I ran straight into the burning cabin, with no idea what I planned to do once I go there. Coughing and choking, I grabbed up the fire extinguisher which I kept by the door and stumbled back out into the night. I threw the fire extinguisher to my landlord as I fell coughing at his feet.

Between the fire extinguisher and the buckets of water hauled from a nearby pond, we got the fire out. But one whole wall of the cabin was gone. Black burn marks crawled their way up the other walls. I was devastated. I curled up in my smoke-soaked blankets and slept in the half-burned cabin.

I began the long process of scrubbing the cabin clean. My friend, Curry offered to rebuild the missing wall, trading it to me for homemade bread. I stayed in what was left of the cabin for three weeks as we worked to put things to right but by the time it was finished, I was cold, and I was tired, and I knew I couldn't live out the rest of the winter there. I began looking for an easier place to land. I could no longer handle the riggers of this life. Winter was setting in and I finally had to admit to myself that even without the fire, I could not have made it through the winter up there alone. It had been magical but the danger I had looked for to force me to overcome was right around the corner and I was not going to overcome it.

A few weeks later, I loaded Two-Bits into a horse trailer, and we carefully made our way down the hill to Denver and beyond. We would move into an old stone house on a ninety-acre property near my summer camp which had been bought by one of the board of directors of the camp and was offered to me for a time. I would help them remodel the place and they would let me live there, on ninety acres of fenced pasture with an old barn, backing up to wilderness areas with lots of trails for riding. I was excited as I pulled into the little circular driveway off the main road. I was relieved. The fire had really been very traumatic, and this place called to me to rest and heal.

CHAPTER 8

Loving Life

I Had electricity. Running water. A gas stove for heat. The house had been in a movie once, a Robert Redford film I barely knew called *Downhill Skier*. The house was quirky and beautiful, made of stone, and such a relief after the trauma of the fire. I settled Two-Bits in the pasture with the old wooden barn and myself into the old stone house. I rested a few weeks, recovering from the harshness of cabin living, and then I began to think. I was trading out rent for help remolding the house. I would paint and put up wallpaper and install new lights. That would keep my expenses down. But we would still need some money. How was I going to support us in this little house on this mountain side? I conceived of a plan.

I would take seven horses from camp during the winter months and rent them out to boarders for a year. During that year, I would teach each client everything they needed to know to have a horse of their own. By then I had become an expert at horse ownership and one of the things I had learned was that adult beginners were rarely prepared when they first got a horse. I knew I could teach them well the things they needed to know to avoid the mistakes I had made. I would return the horses to camp for the summers in better shape than they would have been if they had run wild all winter. And I would have a business to run.

Despite the fire and the hardship of my cabin life, I had thrived in many ways. My health had improved. It would not have stayed improved had I spent the winter in my cabin, I knew that. But for the months that I was there the peace and quiet mixed with just a little bit of hard work had improved my health a great deal. Enough so that I could imagine that running a horse ranch by myself was not only possible, but a very fine idea.

***

I had students, a few local adults and a handful of girls from Columbine High School, who would come to the ranch every weekend and periodically throughout the week. Someone brought a canvas tent and an old wood stove, and they all brought their families and spent the winter days taking turns riding each other's horses, having barbeques, and talking about horse things from dawn until dusk and sometimes beyond. The girls sat at my kitchen table drinking hot chocolate and talked about their dreams and their problems and their frustrations with school. Then we rode horses until dark in the deep snow around the ranch.

Twice I started dating Dave again, long distance. He would fly me out to Chicago and a friend would watch my ranch for a week. I loved those weeks. But always in the back of my mind I felt guilt. I knew I wasn't in this for the long term, and I felt like I was taking advantage of him. I was using him for the ease and pleasure I got from being in his world, but I knew that ultimately, I would always go back to my world. Eventually the guilt would be too much, and I would break up with him again. Then we'd start talking once more and I would go and visit him and…

I was sure he wasn't right for me. But I couldn't let him go.

***

For two years Two-Bits and I lived on our ranch in Colorado, caring for our herd and teaching our students. I got a German Shepherd puppy whom Two-Bits loved to torment, chasing him around the pasture and always just barely avoiding catching him. Poor Rajah learned to mistrust those four-legged beasts I spent so much time with, but he stayed by my side even so.

Rajah was the partner every dog-person dreams of. He seemed to understand everything I said. I could talk to him, telling him to stay behind me or get in the car or whatever I needed him to do, and he'd do it without hesitation whether he had ever heard those words before or not. He lived for me, followed my every command, was my shadow. From day one I required him to do a down stay every time I sat down to a meal, taught him to go to his bed on command and follow me everywhere. As he grew, his feet got big and he would run in an awkward gait, often tripping over his own paws. His ears, which didn't stand up yet, would both flop over one of his eyes, so that he was forever throwing back his head to clear them out of his line of sight. He wasn't afraid of anything except the horses, and he loved everyone.

For the first year at the ranch, I reveled in the life I had created for myself. I had friends, a business that I loved, a dog and a horse. And I loved my little stone house, though I soon discovered that I was not very good at painting or finish work or any of the other remolding jobs I was supposed to be doing in exchange for rent. Oh, I tried. I just didn't have the skills.

So, I lived at my horse ranch in Colorado, hiking for long hours in the hills around my home, teaching riding lessons and caring for all my horses. I loved every minute of it and, true to form, I threw myself into it without concern. How could something I loved this much hurt me, after all? But it did.

A year into living at the ranch, my body started to give out again. Once again, as I pushed myself from dawn till dusk, I started collapsing in random places, my energy gone. I would push all day, ignoring the pain in my lungs which always warned that my energy was being stretched too thin. Then I would start to get dizzy as I went about my day, start to experience the world as if through a long tunnel. Around the edges, my vision would blur and go black. I would collapse and I would lay somewhere for hours before someone found me and helped me back to bed.

One afternoon after a particularly intense snowstorm, I was struggling to get from the house to the barn to feed the horses. The snow had drifted 3-4 feet deep across the bottom of my pasture and I was struggling to push my way to the old barn 100 feet up a hill behind the house. Shaking, I pushed and pushed but ultimately my body gave out. I collapsed in the snow just short of the barn. As snow caved in around me, I knew I was in trouble. Then the world went black.

The next thing I remember was Rajah's insistent bark. Over and over, right in my face he barked, dragging me back from unconsciousness. "Go away," I begged, "Just leave me be." But he wouldn't go away.

Finally, his bark became so insistent I couldn't ignore it anymore. "All right!" I told him, "All right!" and I drag myself back from unconsciousness. But I was too weak to stand, too weak to fight my way the last few feet to the barn. I struggled to get up but when I couldn't do it, I sank back down into the snow, my eyes slipping closed, my gray winter cape falling around me. Then I felt a tug. Rajah had my hood in his teeth, and he was pulling, pulling as hard as he could, trying to drag me on. Every few seconds he would stop and bark, aggressively in my ear, insisting that I wake up and try again. He got me to the barn through some mix of his pulling and his cajoling and as I crawled inside, he snuggled up close to me where I lay in a deep pile of hay, and he laid his nose on my chest. He kept watch through that day and into the night as I slept the sleep of the dead. The next morning, I stumbled my way to the house, asked a friend to feed the horses for me for a bit and slept for three days straight.

After that I trained the horses to come meet me at the gate every time I went to feed. They would swim through the deep snow, their mains and tails dragging on the snow that reached their chests, and I would climb up on a fencepost and jump onto Burt's back. Burt was a big red horse, solid like a draft in many ways, who was the head of my herd. I would cling to his back, my knees brushing the snow, as he and his fellows swam their way back to the barn where I would feed them, then use the path they had plowed to make my way home. Always, Rajah followed behind.

After one of my collapses, I would take a week or so to recover fully, or maybe not completely fully. More and more the fatigue was constant, worse sometimes and better others but always there, in my chest, like an ache. Once I was better, I would go back to pushing myself to care for my horses, hike

76

my mountains and teach my students. I ignored the pain and fatigue, pushing it away and forcing myself to go on. My anger had come back, anger at not being able to manage this life that I loved, and I refused to slow down.

Later that winter I was hiking in the hills around my home. My ranch backed up to an open space park with hundreds of acres of tree-covered trails. I loved to hike those trails, deep into the mountains, the snow falling down. One day I set out with Rajah beside me and was two miles in when the soft snow turned hard. The wind picked up and the snow started falling in sheets, fast and furious around me. And it seemed I had misjudged my energy that day. The fatigue came on fast, like the storm. As the wind and snow whipped at me, I struggled down the trail towards home, but knew I wasn't going to make it. I collapsed in the snow and this time I knew there was no barn to drag me to, no shelter to find. As the world went black, I felt fear and panic as if from a long distance, trying to get through to my muddled brain.

I only remember pieces of what happened next. I was in and out of consciousness and got the story in bits over the next couple hours. Apparently, Rajah left me and made his way to the highway which ran past the open space park next to our ranch. Somehow, he stopped a car on that road and convinced a man to follow him up the trail to find me. The man was young, with long hair. He just kept saying, "I couldn't turn around. He wouldn't let me turn around and I knew, I just knew that it was real." I think he was as astonished by the whole thing as I was. He followed Rajah into the woods and found me and, through a combination of carrying me and helping me walk on my own, he got me home. When we reached home, he settled me onto my couch, fussing around uncomfortably with no idea what to do. I was in and out of consciousness but eventually came to enough to explain my illness and convinced him that I was okay now. Eventually he left and I fell into a deep sleep on my couch. I didn't even know his name.

That collapse took weeks to recover from and my energy never fully came back.

As time went on, I got worse. I was in constant pain. My mind began to slip; confusion and brain fog would hit me like a brick until I barely knew where I was some days. I would force myself out to feed the horses, barely managing to stumble back into the house and collapse on the living room floor. I would lay there until evening when I would drag myself back out to feed again. At home, I was too tired to clean up after myself, and so dishes piled up around the house, with rotting food still on them. I barely managed to feed myself and I never rode my horses anymore. Once things got that bad, it was only a matter of time.

***

My Dad came out that spring to try and help me keep my ranch life alive. His wife, Ruth Ann, whom I had never appreciated, came with him, and the minute she arrived she went to work. She cleaned. She cooked. She put meals in the freezer for me. She did my dishes and scrubbed my floors. She did it all like it was nothing, just something that needed to be done. And she never asked for thanks.

I thanked her anyway. This was the first time I really began to see the value in this woman who lived to care for others, the value I had overlooked for years. She was a gift. She allowed me to extend my time at the ranch by months that year, putting off the inevitable end to this life I loved. But end it must. Because my energy was not getting better. It was getting ever worse.

***

Eventually I had to close my horse ranch down. I sent the horses back to camp and Two-Bits I moved next door to a professional boarding stable because I could no longer make it out to feed her twice a day. Rajah and I barely managed to find food for ourselves and once again the dishes piled up and the fruit flies gathered. Eventually my friends sat me down. "You can't go on like this," they told me. "You have to call your mother." So, I did. There was just one thing I had to deal with first.

78

I knew that this crash wasn't like the times when I had collapsed in the woods or fallen in the horse pasture: get me to safety and give me a couple of weeks of rest and I would be back on my feet. I was way past that now. This would take months, maybe a year or more to get me to the point where I could take care of myself again. I could feel it in my bones, how deep this went. And I knew I couldn't own a horse. Two-Bits needed more than this, to stand in a stall all day waiting for me to come to her. She needed a rider who could keep up with her, a rider who could be safe with her. And one of my students, who had also become a friend, was just such a rider. She had passed me by in skill and was working with horses professionally. I gave her my horse and my time in Colorado was done.

My mother came to get me on a sunny spring day, packing me up in the back of her little red hatch back and driving me back to Michigan. This time I didn't settle into the upstairs room with the shelves for my herbs. It was too hard to walk up the stairs. They put me instead in a downstairs room right by the bathroom and the kitchen. They tucked me into bed, and I lay there mourning the loss of my Colorado life.

***

I was 26 and living at my mother's house again, after having lost my wild, outdoor life in Colorado. I was struggling even to sit up or walk across a room. Around this time, I aged out of my mother's health insurance. I began relying on free clinics for my health care. And I wanted care. During my time in Colorado, I had kept doctors to a minimum, convinced I could overcome this illness through will power or grace. But now I was again desperate for someone to figure out what was wrong and fix it. I searched for a doctor who could help.

Most of the doctors ignored my cries for help or prescribed antidepressants. They told me I was lazy or depressed or that I just needed to buck up and try. One day as I sat being examined by one of them my body began to shake from the effort to hold myself up in a sitting position. He looked at me in surprise. "Are you afraid?" he asked, in confusion.

"No," I said, "it just takes so much energy to hold myself up in a sitting position. I just have trouble sitting up for this long." He looked at me in surprise and began asking more questions. Finally, he sat me down and spoke frankly to me.

"Look," he said, "I can see that there is something very wrong with you. I can see that it is not depression or laziness or any of those things. But the truth is, I can't help you. Free clinics are not set up to deal with an illness like yours. No one here will ever be able to offer you anything but antidepressants not because we think that is the answer but because that is the best we are equipped to do in this environment." So, I saved up my money and got an appointment with a rheumatologist in town. Only one appointment—I didn't have the money for anything more. But if he could just diagnose me, tell me what was wrong, then maybe…maybe…someone somewhere could help me.

Everything was riding on this one visit. And I was so stressed out about it that I couldn't eat the day before. I felt beaten down by all the doctors who insisted it was all in my head, I was lazy or just trying to scam the system. I didn't know how to keep this doctor from thinking the same.

I was so stressed that the minute I walked into the waiting room, I burst into tears. By the time I got to his office, I was sobbing so hard I couldn't speak. Unsurprisingly, he diagnosed me with depression, told me to move out of my mother's house and sent me on my way.

For a long time, I stayed in bed, searching my mind and heart for some scrap of hope, something that would make the future worth dreaming of again.

***

I was tucked in tight beneath a pink and gray quilt amidst soft pillows with a window overlooking the yard. The wood floors were dark, and colorful throw rugs dotted my path to the door and the bathroom beyond. I lay in that bed for weeks, too tired even to watch TV or read a book. I lay there and I thought about the life I had just lost. And for the first time in my life, I entertained the possibility that this illness might never go away.

I looked at my life, this laying in bed, weak and unable to take care of myself, and I asked, "What if this is all there is?"

"What if I never have more than I have right now?"

"How can I ever be content with only this for the rest of my life?"

And ultimately it came to me. I couldn't. I couldn't find a way to be content with this life. But I couldn't stop living either. I considered that in all seriousness. Did I want to end my life, move on, try for something new? I didn't. There were too many ties anchoring me to this life, too many people that I loved who would be devastated by such a blow. I had walked that path once as a teenager, and suicide would never be an option for me again. I couldn't go forward, and I couldn't go back. That left only one thing. If I couldn't be naturally content with this life, somehow, I had to find a way to be *unnaturally* content with it.

"Alright," I decided. "Here is how it's going to be. Every day I will have a treat: A new book or set of markers, a piece of my favorite candy, a particularly good meal. And as long as I have my treat, I will be happy. I will love life. I will have a *good day*."

And it worked. Almost instantly it worked. Each day I picked a treat. At first it was mostly a small food item, since I had no income and buying a treat wasn't often feasible for me. (Even a $5.00 marker set was usually out of my reach at that point.) It didn't have to be much. Maybe just a single tootsie roll. As long as I fixated on it and looked forward to it and paid close attention to enjoying it to the fullest, I was suffused with a sense of well-being. For the rest of the day, I had a gentle feeling of joy glowing in the core of me: A feeling of loving life, of great appreciation for everything I had, an acute awareness of my blessings. The effect was not just psychological. It was physical. When I got my treat, my body would release a rush of endorphins which lasted me the rest of the day. It would be years before I understood that I had created a made-to-order addiction for myself. All I knew at the time was that it worked.

***

Slowly, I began to get better. Months passed before I could walk on my own to the living room sofa. More months passed before I could go out in the yard. It was a year before I could walk around the block. But as I reached that milestone, I began, once again, to think of my future.

I wouldn't be able to hold a job. But maybe, with the little bit of money my mother and brother gave me every month, I could find a room to rent to give me some feeling of independence. And I could sell my herbs to earn a little more. Meanwhile, Dave had started visiting again and we had picked up where we left off. I loved being with him. I loved the freedom I felt, the way he cared for me, and I loved going places on his arm. I was proud to be seen with him in his well-groomed beard and broad shoulders. But some part of me still felt guilty about it. Was I using him for the ease he lent to my life? Was it fair to him that I loved the financial freedom he lent me when we were together? Should I just end it again and let us both move on?

I was staying with a friend, visiting one of my best friends now that I was finally able, with some difficulty, to travel again. And I voiced my doubts. His response took me entirely by surprise.

"For God's sake!" he said. "You need to get your act together. You have waffled around this man for years, stringing him along, but you have never really given him a chance. You have always been convinced that it wouldn't work between you. Either give it a real chance for once or let the man go for real this time. He deserves better than this."

I was shocked. It was like a slap in the face to be talked to that way by my friend. But as the shock wore off, I realized something: he was right. I had never really given Dave a chance. I had been convinced from the start that he wasn't right for me and held back because of it. Dave did deserve better than this.

I talked to Dave on the phone that night. "Look," I said, "I have been convinced from the start that we could never work together. And I never wanted to take advantage of you by making you believe in me and then breaking up with you. So, I have held back all this time, never really letting myself go and seeing what I feel about you." I told him about what Jim had said. "I think he's right. I want to try this again and this time I won't hold back. But I need you to know that I give you no guarantees. It might turn out just the way I fear and end with me leaving you for good. But if you are willing to take that risk, then I will try it one more time, for real this time." And he said yes.

I fell in love.

I fell completely in love.

The minute I stopped holding back, I was hit by such a rush of love for this man that I could hardly contain it all. And I saw clearly for the first time: Dave was perfect for me. That cowboy I had been waiting for. That would have been a disaster. If anyone was designed to help me get the best out of my life it was Dave. Like he had been made specifically for me—and me for him.

I always jumped into life with both feet, running full tilt at everything I loved. My body couldn't take that and ultimately, I lost the thing I loved because of it. Dave was cautious, perhaps too cautious. But together we balanced each other out. I slowed down enough to make better choices, choices that I could sustain. He sped up enough to experience life and overcome his fears. He pulled me back, I pulled him forward, and somehow along the way we both ended up at a much healthier pace.

Gone was my guilt, my worry that I was using him. Yes, I loved the financial stability he brought to my life. Yes, I loved the care he took of me. But I also just loved him. Dave was strong and solid, funny and at ease. He was a rare computer program with social skills. I was proud to introduce him to my friends and family. I was proud to be seen with him. We could talk long into the night about subjects that interested me, philosophy and politics, religion, and life after death. He was interested in self-improvement, though he had never focused much on that area of his life before. And he loved me. Despite all my need, he loved me.

It became apparent very quickly that our days of breaking up and starting over were done. I still wasn't interested in marriage, but I was interested in him, and for the long term. Once he saw that this was true, he asked me to move in with him. He offered to buy us a house in the suburbs of Chicago where Rajah could run, and to support me in every way. If I wanted to go back to school, get my degree after all these years, he would support me in that as well.

We bought a two-story white house with black shutters in Lisle, Illinois, right outside of Naperville where I would attend North Central College. Our house backed up to a park and was bordered by a creek. We had a big back yard which we promptly fenced in. The night we moved in we laid down blankets on our new bedroom floor and ordered take-out. I was excited about yet another adventure—one that felt bigger and more important than any of the other adventures I'd had. The moving truck would come the next day.

Section Three

Strip Malls And Big Box Stores

27 years old – 35 years old…

We must be ready to let go of the life we've planned, so as to have the life that is waiting for us.

(Joseph Campbell)

CHAPTER 9

Growing Up

W hen I was in grade school, I dreamed of being a fireman. Oh, and a teacher and a zookeeper, an airplane pilot, a famous writer, an actress, a policeman and a cowboy. Then I grew up and went to junior high school.

When I was in junior high school, I dreamed of being president. Oh, and stopping all suffering, bringing justice to the world, ending hunger and wars, and creating a utopia upon the earth. Then I grew up and went to high school.

When I was in high school, I dreamed of being a congresswoman before I ran for president, just to give myself a little practice at the job. And I began to plan how I would end suffering and bring happiness to the world. Then I met suffering and pain myself. And I grew up.

A college degree had been my first adult goal, left undone when my illness set me on a different path. Now, living in Chicago with Dave, I returned to that goal.

I had recovered enough to walk around the block, back at my mother's house in Michigan. But my energy didn't stretch much further than that. I could run a few errands, assuming I had a handicapped flag to make parking easy and keep the walking to a minimum, but I would be exhausted and shaky by the end of it. Coming home I would fall into bed and sleep for hours before I would painstakingly get up and unpack the bags I had brought.

But I wanted to finish school. Many people asked me why I was bothering to get my degree. I was no more likely to be able to hold a job after graduating than before. I tried to explain that I had the need to accomplish something I had set out to do. I'd had too many setbacks, courtesy of this illness, over the years. I needed to see a success, no matter what it took.

What it took was a lot of help.

Each quarter was a struggle. I spent time in the hospital and sometimes had to be carried out of class. I usually had to take every other quarter off, and I went half-time as a matter of course.

When I was younger, I had believed that I would spend my life giving to others, helping others. Instead of giving to others, I lay in bed, unable to make my own food; unable to do my own laundry. Instead of giving I was the one in need. I could choose to accept this help and have some chance of accomplishing this goal I had set out for myself. Or I could try to go it alone and fail.

So, I lay in my bed, and I accepted help. I used a handicapped sticker to park closer to the buildings I needed to enter. I let Dave do the grocery shopping and make our meals. I asked my mother to come, once a month, to help keep up with projects around the house. I welcomed only guests who could look after themselves, not needing to be waited on, who could pitch in and help out while they were here. I built a community.

The third time I attempted college, I chose North Central College, in Naperville, Illinois, a school which was actively committed to making education accessible to students with disabilities. They started by assigning me a personal representative from their Disabilities Services Office. That person evaluated what I would need to succeed at graduating and set about making it happen. She talked to professors, the Dean of Students, and the Campus Health Center. I was introduced to all the security guards on campus so that when they found me passed out on the way to my car, they would know who I was and what to do for me. Though I lived only a few miles from campus, the school gave me my own room in the Health Center for sleeping when I was too tired to drive home. My representative got me all my books on tape so that I could listen to them when I was too weak to read.

One day, midway through a term, I found myself stumbling towards my next class when I realized I was not going to make it. I was just walking past the Dean of Students office when the fatigue hit, so I staggered towards her door, fell to the ground, and crawled into her outer office. The secretary shrieked and jumped up in a panic. The Dean of Students stuck her head out of her office to see what all the commotion was about and, seeing me on the floor, addressed the other people in the office. "It's all right," she said calmly, "It's only Christie!"

She asked two bystanders to lift me up and carry me into an empty conference room. They laid me on a couch and tucked a pillow under my head, letting me lay there until I regained my strength. Once I could sit up, the Dean came in and asked me what class I was trying to get to. She then walked me to my class and made sure I was settled before going back to her normal day's work.

It sometimes seemed that everyone at North Central pitched in to help me get my college degree.

Some days I had to lie down in the back of my classroom and listen to lectures from the floor because I was too tired to sit up in a chair. Once a professor came to my house to bring me homework and explain a tricky concept when I had a bad spell and hadn't been able to get to class that week.

I don't know if it was luck or grace that landed me at this school where they had such an astounding commitment to helping students like me. I had decided to get this degree and whatever it took, I was committed. But I couldn't have done it if they weren't equally as committed to this goal.

I went to North Central College for four years, making my graduation a total of eleven years since I had first started college. I had never been able to hold a regular job and I likely never would. But I have never regretted getting my degree. I needed to see that I could, no matter the effort, accomplish something I set out to do. It was important that I knew that this was possible. It was the next step in the process of growing up.

***

For four years, I lived in Chicago with Dave.

Two-Bits still belonged to my friend, Kelly. I hadn't seen them since I moved out of Colorado. I had returned after the Columbine shootings to visit with my students and hear them talk about hiding in cabinets in libraries or under tables in cafeterias as two shooters killed their friends around them. I had not been back since and had not written Kelly in many months to hear the latest news about Two-Bits. I was trying to stay away from them, trying not to interfere with their relationship or cause Kelly to feel like Two-Bits was still mine. I wanted Two-Bits to be hers completely. They both deserved that kind of bond.

I missed the bond I had had with Two-Bits. I missed it terribly. But I knew that I couldn't handle a horse right now and I knew that even if I could, Two-Bits was still above my skill level. So, I hung her picture next to my bed and tried to support her in having a better life with someone else, no matter how much that hurt my heart. And part of that support was staying out of their way as they bonded to each other.

But Two-Bits was on my mind. She was often on my mind, but this was different. I had woken up some nights before feeling strongly that Two-Bits needed me, and I had not been able to get her out of my mind since. I was trying to stay away, not infringe on the relationship Kelly was building with her. So, I avoided calling. But I couldn't let it go.

Finally, I wrote to Kelly. "*I don't want to get in the way of your doing whatever you think is best for Two-Bits and you together. But I just had to write. I woke up some nights ago feeling like she needed me, and I have not been able to shake the feeling since. So, I'd love an update on how she is doing, and I want to make sure you know that if anything ever changes in your life and you can't care for her, I will always take her back. I will always find a way to make sure that she is okay. I know it's a lot to have put on you, the expenses of a horse and all. If you need help with her or feel she is no longer a good fit for you, I trust you to find the home you want for her but barring that I will always be willing to do what is needed to make sure she is cared for."*

I got a letter back.

"I couldn't write you," Kelly said, *"And I couldn't call. I didn't know how to tell you. A couple of weeks ago Two-Bits colicked. We had the vet out. We did everything we could. But she didn't make it. There was nothing we could do."*

I sat for hours with the letter in my hand, staring into space until Dave convinced me to come to bed. That horse had carried my heart for years. And she took a piece of it with her when she left this world for good.

* * *

As I came to Chicago and this house in the suburbs, I found that I had left something more than the mountains and the falling stars and the snow that still comes down in June. I had left my dream life behind me, and yet, somehow, the old life still surrounded me and would not let me go. The pieces of it hovered around my vision, in my thoughts, in my writing. They came out as images of moments and places and people, to emerge in small scenes woven into stories here and there.

Sometimes it seemed that my whole life had been a series of emergencies, responded to desperately in the heat of the moment. That had been my choice, I know. I had lived for passion and excitement, always seeking drama in the world. And there was no greater drama than seeing life and death laid out before you and knowing that it is your wit, your skill, your strength alone that would decide which came.

Those years were defined by the adrenaline I lived on to get through them. They were defined by images; the night of flames and desperate trips to a pond to fill buckets with water as my cabin burned; by guns and chipped steel knives in angry, weathered hands. There were so many days, so many hours spent struggling to survive.

I had lived my whole life on fast forward, believing life to be that rush of adrenaline that quickens the heart and speeds up the mind, heightening awareness and passions until all else falls away. And then I'd stopped. I'd married a man and moved to a house in the suburbs. I traded in the emergencies and the desperate excitement of risk for grass to be mowed and gardens to play in and gentle rivers to be watched from lawn chairs on brick patios while steaks cooked on the grill. It was as though I, who had always run through life, was suddenly standing still.

And the truth is, I was quite content. More than that. I was at peace.

"Chicago," the last place on earth I ever dreamed of putting down roots: exceedingly unglamorous compared to the places I had lived before. "House in the suburbs" was never a phrase I thought to claim.

And yet, I was happy here—happier than I had been in a long, long time. It was a quiet kind of happiness, a deep kind, and nothing like the euphoric rush I knew as happiness before. I wanted this life. I wanted this gentleman who came home from work every evening and woke me from my nap. I wanted this picket fence and deep green yard and the white garage with the broken garage-door opener. I wanted the herb garden, the compost pile and the recycling bins which had to be taken to the curb every Tuesday night.

I loved the quirky home-repairs which never seem to end. I loved playing Frisbee with my dog in the city park. I loved the gentleness, the stillness of this life. And yet, as I settled into it with such relief, as I sat in it and learned the remarkable feeling of stillness, I found myself haunted by the memories of the life I had lived. I was where I needed to be. What was I to do with all the places which I had brought with me? How could I honor the richness of those years, while at the same time leaving them behind?

I took up my pen and notebook and sat cross-legged on the weathered bench in my backyard, and gazed a bit at the brilliant pink flowers which covered my trees. I wrote of teepees and mountain men and waking from sleep to the sound of a bear or meeting a lion on a mountain trail. And my heart lived the memories. Then I left my bench to go inside to vacuum or do laundry, and in the evening, I greeted my gentle man, putting images of bears and mountain lions out of my mind, as we drove past shopping malls to meet friends at Sushi bars or pay too much for popcorn at movie-theaters with thirty screens.

Chapter 10

Life With Dave

Living with Dave was a gift. And over time I began to think more and more about marriage. Not because I wanted a better name to call him by. Not because I was looking for some way to express my love. I started thinking of marriage because I wanted that kind of commitment with Dave. I wanted to offer him a sacred promise that we would stand together, build a life together, forever, as long as we both shall live. I began to see that there was value in that which I'd never recognized before.

It isn't that we couldn't have gone on living together for the rest of our lives and done fine with that. I trusted our commitment to each other. But I wanted something more. And I began to understand that marriage was that something more. I knew in some way I couldn't articulate that marriage was not just a legal status, but a journey you took with another human being. A journey of personal growth. And I wanted that journey.

Dave and I both came from divorced parents. And I felt that those divorces had been justified, good even. They had been the best thing for all involved. But I also knew that when I married, divorce would not be an option. Marriage was an all-in proposition for me. And I knew that I could approach it that way, in part, because I knew what I was signing up for. I wasn't looking for happiness, though I hoped that would come. I was looking for growth. And I knew, also, that I had the right foundation. I had found a man who cared as much about my happiness as he did about his own and I felt the same. It's amazing how many people don't have that basic prerequisite going into a marriage. Without it, I don't know how you would ever make a marriage work.

But as I became aware of this, I was also aware that Dave hadn't thought these things out to the extent that I had. If we got married, he would not be signing up for the same thing I would.

I turned to Dave one evening as we puttered around our room before bed. We had talked a lot about marriage, and he knew that I was not interested in that. I knew that he was, or thought he was. "Dave," I said, "I think I am ready to get married. But I don't think you are. I don't think you fully understand what marriage means to me and until we are both on the same page, it won't work." He listened. We talked. He agreed—he had never thought so deeply about what marriage meant. Marriage was simply marriage. We decided to go to a counselor together to sort all this out, get us both on the same page and check in with each other to make sure we were both going into this with eyes wide open. We went to a half a dozen counseling sessions together and then Dave went alone for a time. One of the things we agreed upon was that if we were to get married, our financial relationship had to change. Up until then, Dave's money was Dave's money. He earned it. He spent it. I influenced that spending quite a bit, but ultimately it was Dave's decision.

I knew that finances in a relationship define a good bit of the power structure of that relationship. I knew I would never earn money to pay for our life, that all of that would come from Dave. But if we were going to marry, then I wanted us to be on an equal footing in every way we could. All of our money would belong to both of us equally. Oh, we could set aside some money for each of us to spend on our own things when we wanted to, but the bulk of it we had to share. Ultimately, Dave agreed. We would make money decisions together. We would share what Dave earned equally. We decided to start changing our financial relationship immediately. We would create a budget together and go from there.

* * *

Dave had finished working with the counselor. We both knew we wanted to get married someday, but I didn't give it much more thought than that. I knew Dave was too busy at work these days to think about rings and proposals. He worked late and came home tired. We spent most of our time together when he wasn't at work. There just wasn't time for him to arrange anything.

It was December and a Christmas tree was sparkling in our living room. I loved Christmas and played Christmas music on Dave's Bose radio. Dave worked for a financial firm that made tons of money. They had planned a glorious office Christmas party for their people that year. They had rented out the Field Museum in downtown Chicago where the full skeleton of a tyrannosaurus rex hangs from the ceiling. We would have dinner and dance under the watchful eyes of "Sue" the dinosaur skeleton. It was an open bar and black-tie night. Dave got a tuxedo. I got an evening gown. It was going to be glorious, and I was really looking forward to it.

In order to save my energy, and as a treat, we rented a hotel room across from the Field Museum. That afternoon, a limo picked me up and took me to the hotel where I rested and began to dress. Dave arrived after work and quickly took a shower. As I was putting on the finishing touches of my make-up, I turned to Dave, now dressed in his tux and looking fine. I slid two bracelets onto one hand and stood for him. "Does this look unbalanced?" I asked, unsure if I should move one of the bracelets over to the other hand. He tilted his head, considering me carefully. "You know, it does." He said.

"Oh, should I move these?" I asked, touching the bracelets.

"Actually," he said, reaching into his vest pocket, "I thought maybe you could add this." And he pulled out a ring. He got down on one knee and proposed.

* * *

95

I was astonished. *How had he pulled that off? When had he gotten a ring?* The ring was specially made, designed by him with a pear-shaped diamond that was protected by a strong setting. Just what was needed for someone who liked to ride horses and spend time out of doors. I couldn't have loved it more.

(I said yes, of course.)

When I finally got my breath back, I asked him, "How did you *do* that? How did you know that I would ask the right thing to set you up like that? What if I hadn't asked??"

He kissed my hand. "Oh, I knew," he told me, "I knew that at some point in getting dressed you would turn to me and ask for my opinion. You always do."

We made our way in a daze to the Field Museum, showing off my ring to everyone. We ate and drank and danced all night.

* * *

Dave has never wavered from the decision he made to treat his money as ours equally. Never once has he said that he regretted this. But what we didn't know at the time was that I had a major problem with money. I had an addiction to spending.

At first, living with Dave it had seemed like money was infinite. We had more discretionary income than I had ever had in my life. We bought a time share. We went out to dinner. We took a vacation in Mexico. And then I started getting credit card offers in the mail. And I accepted them because, why not? Soon I had a dozen credit cards. And soon they were all full.

I hardly knew how it happened. I would get home from the store thinking I had spent $50-$60 and find that I had spent $600. Pretty soon we owed so much on credit cards that we had to struggle to pay our basic bills. We agreed that we had to stop going out to eat so much, had to stop being so extravagant. But any time I started to feel grief at the state of my body, any time I had a really hard day, I would go out and buy something in order to feel okay again. It didn't matter that we'd agreed not to do that. I did it anyway. I couldn't stop myself.

One night in Chicago Dave and I were trying to decide what to have for dinner. I wanted Thai food. I *really* wanted Thai food. But we both knew that we needed to stop eating out so much.

I started to pace back and forth. I started to rant. I wanted Thai food; I couldn't have Thai food. I could hardly breathe. I was in tears and panicked. I hated life. I couldn't do this anymore.

I frightened Dave. He had never seen me like this. I couldn't explain what was wrong. I didn't know. I just knew that my life suddenly felt not worth living. Really *not worth living*. I got worse and worse, escalating my panic and my misery. Finally, he said, "Okay, okay. Let's get Thai food. We'll get Thai food. It's okay."

Instantly I was fine again. All my agitation was gone. I couldn't remember what had seemed so wrong with life. My life was wonderful.

Now Dave was really scared. This was just crazy. What was going on?

I didn't know. And at that moment, I wasn't all that concerned about it. I was getting my Thai food. Life was good. Life was *great*. What reason did I have to be concerned? I was euphoric. But even through my euphoria I saw how freaked out Dave was. And some part of me recognized that something was really not right with this situation. I started trying to understand what had happened.

We began to notice things we hadn't seen before. I became obsessive about eating out or ordering in just the right food, regularly. It didn't matter how tight money was. I had to have my treat. We hadn't seen it before because we rarely tried to deny me when I wanted it that badly. But now we were seeing it and seeing it everywhere. Because it wasn't just a matter of food. When I was having a hard day, I would go out and buy make-up or art supplies or new pillows for the couch. I knew we didn't have the money for those things. I knew we had agreed to talk to each other before we bought anything. But still, I did it. And those few times when I tried to restrain myself, I became agitated, panicked, and upset all out of proportion.

The effects were physical, not just emotional. When I got my treat, I was flooded with endorphins, my heartbeat slowed, and I couldn't help but smile. And I was so happy with my life it was difficult for me, at those times, to remember why I had ever been unhappy with it before. After all, what was an illness compared to this *joy* I felt?

When I didn't get my treat, my hands got clammy. My heartbeat sped up. I became short of breath, my stomach cramped, I felt panicked. I felt like my life was in danger. Like not having this treat was a threat to my very survival. And I felt like I couldn't continue with this awful life I was living.

We didn't understand this. We didn't see the patterns yet or know anything about addictions. I would commit to being more careful with money and manage that for a while but then I would have a really hard day and I couldn't help it. I bought something. I bought everything. And pretty soon we were cashing in Dave's investments to pay off our credit cards, then filling them all up again. And we didn't know why.

***

I graduated on a lovely day in May. My whole family came to cheer me on. Dave was right there beside me. We'd been married for a year. I was proud. I was elated.

I was also exhausted from my last semester, worn out and in pain. I rested through the rest of May and June. When finally, I began to be able to function again, I gathered my camping supplies and packed a bag for Rajah. I wanted to live somewhere out west. We had come to see that my health was always better when I lived in the mountain climate of Colorado. A number of times through my Chicago years, I had taken a couple of months and gone to

Colorado where Rajah and I hiked for weeks on end, living on our own in the mountains. I went from barely being able to drive myself around Chicago to carrying a full pack and hiking every day. And it worked.

Maybe it was the lack of humidity. We noticed that when the humidity in Chicago got bad, I could barely function. Colorado didn't have that kind of humidity. Just stepping into that climate was like shedding a steel ball and chain that hung around my neck for most of my life.

Or maybe it was leaving the city behind. As my energy had become more precious, I had begun to notice just how much energy it takes to live in a city, aware even if only subconsciously, of all the millions of things going on around me. When I walked into the wilderness, it was like I could breathe deeply for the first time. And besides, I was in love with the mountains. I wanted to live in the west, somewhere where we could have some land. Somewhere where I could have horses. I loved Colorado, but anywhere within reach of Denver, where Dave could get a job, would be too expensive. We could never afford horse land around Denver, and we didn't want a long commute for Dave.

Dave was on board with it if we could find the right place. He needed to be able to work. His Chicago job was a good one. But he was employable. He could get work in any big city. And he had begun to notice a kind of negativity that overtook him when he was in the city. He was developing road rage. He didn't like that. We decided that once I'd recovered from my last semester at school, I would drive out west, stopping in towns along the way, looking for a place we both could live.

I would visit Colorado, Wyoming, Oregon, and California. Rajah and I would drive for two months, camping along the way, and see what we could find. July, August and then in September, for our anniversary, Dave and I would meet in Sun Valley Idaho, rent a condo through our time share company and talk about all the places I'd found. We added Montana to the itinerary when, at the last minute, my sister called from a city called Missoula. She and her husband had moved to Missoula, Montana so her husband could go to law school there. "I think you'll like this town," she told us, "I think it's just what you are looking for."

I knew nothing about Montana. Cold and foreboding and more politically conservative than I was willing to settle for, those were my impressions. But I trusted my sister. And she was right.

I loved Missoula immediately. My guidebook called it "the red headed stepchild of Montana." It was a bastion of liberal politics and an active city packed with culture. Good restaurants, theater, social activities for families: it was just the kind of town I'd been hoping for. I contacted a realtor, and she took me all over the area looking at places with a little land attached. None of them seemed quite right.

I sat in the realtor's office one morning as we debated which homes to look at that day. I was flipping through a big 3-ring binder with listings of all kinds. I came across one with a grainy picture of a small log cabin. "This one," I said, "I want to see this one."

"Oh, I don't think you do," she argued. "That is very remote. It is entirely off-grid. I don't think it even has electricity."

"That's it," I told her. "That's the one I want to see."

Three weeks later I met up with Dave in Sun Valley, Idaho to celebrate our anniversary together. I borrowed a slide projector from a nearby university. "This is where I want to live," I told him and I walked him through slides of meadows with vast horse pastures, hillsides covered with trees, a beautiful log cabin and three horse barns. Along with the house and three barns, it had nine fenced pastures, a hay barn, and a greenhouse. A creek ran through it and there was a natural mountain spring up on a hill which piped water down to the house. There was no electricity, but the water was good, and the house was sound.

I had been drawing pictures for years of my dream home: barns and pastures and a little log house. This place fit it exactly. It was remote. The road to get there reminded me of the old winding forest road I drove to get to my cabin outside of Drake, Colorado. Though it was only 9 miles from town, the road seemed to go on and on. You could rarely go 20 miles per hour, at times only 5. There were no street signs up there, and Google maps was not well enough established at that time to reach such a remote place. I fell in love. This was everything I wanted.

The question was, would Dave love it too?

He did. He flew home as I drove east. Over the next couple of months, we talked with the owners, and a bank. Then we flew to Missoula for an in person visit together. And we bought it. An off-grid horse ranch in Montana. We would move in June.

Section Four

A Ranch In Montana

35 years old – 45 years old…

What are you going to do with your one wild and precious life?

(Mary Oliver)

Chapter 11

New Life In Montana

That winter, before we moved to Montana, I began searching for some horses to buy. I was excited. I wanted horses in my life. I knew my energy made it dangerous to work with horses at times, so I went looking for a breed that would give me an edge up; something that wasn't quite so easily spooked, something that would allow me to be safe even when I wasn't at my best. I didn't know if such a breed existed, but I kept hearing about the Rocky Mountain Horse and what I heard was promising. Unbelievable, but promising.

People liked to say the Rocky Mountain Horse was "born broke" and that you could often begin riding a youngster out on the trails without any training at all. Over and over, I heard that they didn't spook at anything, they trusted people and they wanted to be around you as much as you wanted to be around them. It was said that given the choice, they would leave their buddies and their food just to follow a person around the pasture all day. I was dubious, but I set about learning everything I could.

At first, I assumed they would be ugly horses. After all, if everything everyone said was true, how could this breed not be the most popular breed in the world unless there was something wrong with them that no one mentioned. But there wasn't. They were beautiful. And the breed had a coloring that few breeds have, a dark brown body with a flaxen mane and tail. A stunning combination. These were not homely animals. They were everything a person dreams of in a horse.

It turned out their reputation was well deserved as well. It was all true. These were flashy, beautiful horses, with a calm nature and desire to relate to people like I had never seen in a horse before. This was a horse I could ride even when my energy was low. And that part about them being born broke? Over the years I have had occasion to ride an untrained Rocky Mountain Horse on the trails once or twice, and while I think official training is important for a horse's mental development, many of them really can manage being ridden with little to no training. They are just that willing and that stable minded. They don't spook at new things and are happy to do what you ask as long as they understand what that is. I didn't know all this when I went to Colorado to meet my first Rocky Mountain Horses. I was still dubious about them living up to all the hype. But I was hopeful. And I was excited.

We found our horses at Post Rock Ranch, in Colorado, which had been breeding horses for almost thirty years. Dave and I went to visit them. They had an old mare who was the quintessential Rocky Mountain Horse. Nothing phased her and she could carry anyone safely. She had broken her neck once in an accident and held her head a little funny, but we didn't care about that. She was amazing. Her best friend was an unusually levelheaded Arab mare and we bought her as well, not wanting to break the two of them up. And finally, there was the stallion. I hadn't intended to buy a stallion, but I saw his picture and had to meet him. He was small—only 14 hands—but stocky with a crested neck and a curly mane and tail that dragged on the ground. He had a delicate face and a compact body, and his coat was pure black. Stoney was one of the most stunning horses I had ever seen, and I fell in love with him at first sight. Normally a stallion is a totally different ball game from other horses and such a thing would not have been an option for me with my limited energy and shaky health. But the Rocky Mountain breed was truly unusual. Stallions in this breed were often easier to work with than geldings or mares of other breeds.

Good horses aren't cheap: weren't cheap even back then, at least not in this breed. We borrowed some money from my mother and paid her back with our tax return that year.

The owners offered to breed my mares to their other stallion before shipping them off, so that I could have babies the next year that wouldn't be related to Stoney. I bought all three of the horses and arranged for them to be shipped to Montana. They would arrive a few weeks after we did.

* * *

When we arrived in Missoula, the day before the closing, the realtor took us up to the house to do our final walk through. The owner was an older woman who had lived in that house for 30 years with her husband from whom she was recently divorced. We were going to have to do two separate closings because the two of them couldn't be in the same room together. (I later learned that theirs was a volatile marriage and that they had been divorced and remarried to *each other* five times already.)

She stood in the doorway, her weathered hands gripping the door handle. I remember looking down at her hands and wondering if I would have skin that parched and lined after 30 years of living in this place. It made me sad, in a way, to think of my young, smooth skin, wrinkled and leathery like hers. But I knew that this was the life I was choosing, and I chose it willingly, even eagerly, despite that sadness.

As we stepped in the door to the house, it became clear that the owner had not yet begun to pack. "I didn't want to go through all that trouble," she told us, "in case you didn't come." Twenty-four hours before the closing and thirty years' worth of ranch equipment and family heirlooms still filled the house, spilled out of the garage and into the many barns.

The realtor sent us back to our hotel. She called a moving company and stood by the owner's side as her life was packed in boxes. By evening the only thing left was her three horses. "I thought they could just stay here," the woman explained, "until I found somewhere else for them to go." By then we knew enough about this woman to know that she wasn't a particularly kind person. She went out of her way for nobody but expected others to go out of their way for her. The realtor didn't think it was a good idea for us to keep her horses. We had our own horses arriving soon and it didn't seem wise to keep such contact between us when the owner was clearly having trouble letting go. I was pretty sure she had not wanted to leave, but had been unable, at her age, to live in this remote place without the help of her ex-husband, already moved into his new house in town. The horses were moved to a neighbor's property until the owner could find a way to bring them to town, where she would be living from then on.

We managed the closing and drove up the long, bumpy road to our new home. The nine-mile drive took about 40 minutes of slowly making our way over potholes and along this narrow, one-lane road. We pulled down the driveway to the beautiful log cabin that we would call home. My heart fluttered at the drive. I had found the place I wanted to live for the rest of my life, and it was mine.

The next day the moving van couldn't make it up the road, so we hired a U-Haul and transferred everything into it for the drive up.

We knew this new life was what we wanted. But it was an act of faith in many ways. We were living according to the maxim, "Leap, and the net will appear." While Dave could do his job from anywhere, working remotely wasn't very common in those days and his boss hadn't agreed to let him try it yet. We had gotten Dave an apartment in Chicago, near Lake Michigan, where he could walk or take the subway to and from work every day. He took two weeks off so we could do the move together, but then he was going to head back to Chicago while I would stay and start our new lives in Montana.

The house was a one-bedroom log cabin with a half loft that was open to the rest of the house. It had a cute back deck overlooking the yard and a large two-story side deck overlooking a small pond and a fire pit. There was a beautiful little sauna built into the side deck, all covered in mosaic tiles. In the yard was a wooden frame for a greenhouse with greenhouse grade plastic sheeting covering it. There was another, smaller greenhouse built onto the side of the house. I was very excited about the greenhouses. I wanted to sink my hands into the dirt and grow things. I wanted to put down roots. I wanted to make a home and *know* this land.

The yard was lush and green. The pastures were covered in grass with a creek meandering through them. Our land was in a valley midway up the mountain. You started out driving up a canyon, with a drop off into Mill Creek on the right which was sometimes quite steep, and a sheer climb on the left of rocks and cliffs and extreme hillside. For the first six miles, you followed waterfalls and the rushing creek and then, as the road wound into the valley, the land opened up. The valley stretched for four or five miles and there were little homesteads and cabins dotting the landscape every few miles. Then the road started down the other side of this mountain and landed on highway 93 near Arlee, Montana.

We owned 60 acres, and halfway across those sixty acres was a small guest cabin. It had been built under an awning designed for an RV to pull up and attach to the cabin, so one wall of the cabin (the one under the awning) was mostly missing. The house and the cabin both were built with huge logs. I loved everything about them. This was an adventure at its finest. We lit oil lamps for light, ran the wood stove for heat, and slowly made the house our home.

And yes, our lights consisted of oil lamps and a few propane lanterns which we lit as needed. There was no electricity unless we pull-started the old Honda generator on the porch and plugged something into it while it ran.

***

The land came with a chicken coup, so of course we needed chickens. Besides, I wanted the pest control they offered when they free range, eating grasshoppers which would otherwise spring up from every patch of grass like grain being scattered as we walked. McMurry Hatchery out of Iowa was the go-to place to buy day old chicks and as long as I was ordering those, I couldn't resist some ducks, geese and turkeys too. We put the order in the day after we moved and a week later, we got a call at eleven o'clock one night from the main Post Office in Missoula. Dave and I rushed down the hill to pick up our chicks. We held boxes of tiny fuzz balls, all cheeping and stumbling around. The ducks, geese and turkeys were bigger than the chicks but still in their baby fuzz, each species in its own box, and I took turns holding each chick on my lap as Dave drove us home.

For two weeks, Dave and I unpacked the house and walked our land, getting to know the fields and trails through the woods, the animals that lived here and what kind of fish swam in our creek. We got the barns ready for the horses and eventually Dave flew back to Chicago. In the meantime, my mom had arrived to spend the summer, sharing our adventure with us, and helping me to settle in. The reactions of our friends and family to this extreme change in our life was always amusing. It was always either, "Wow! That sounds awesome!" or "Why in the world would you do something like that??" There was no in between. The first summer a family friend called us up and said they just had to check out this new adventure of ours. Could they come and stay for a couple of weeks? Maybe to help me get settled?

I said yes and despite having only one bedroom, me, my mom, and our friends Karen and Aud (short for Audrey) spent a month getting the house put to rights and the barns ready for the horses. Karen and Aud ended up making the ranch a yearly vacation. For the next twenty years they came out every summer, at least once but often twice, and once they retired, they began to stay the whole summer. They eventually bought an RV to keep on our land and to give themselves some space of their own. They bought horses from us as well as a piece of land adjacent to ours. They became a permanent and essential part of the ranch family.

And there was a ranch family. Everyone we knew wanted to check out this new adventure of ours and most of them did. It soon became normal for us to have a house full of guests: friends and family and friends of friends. We opened our doors to everyone, and everyone came. Family came, and friends from Chicago and Denver, but also strangers who knew someone who knew us. Those first few years, we had people from New Zealand,

Germany and Switzerland come spend anywhere between a week and three months, exploring Montana and experiencing what it was like to live on a ranch. We also had people from all over the United States. At times, we would have guests crashed out on the living room floor in sleeping bags or sleeping on the back deck, and we took to making dinners together around the campfire each night, everyone pulling up a log and sitting about, sharing what they had done with their day.

I quickly learned that I loved having guests but couldn't be the traditional hostess that took care of everything and everyone. I just didn't have the energy. But I loved sharing the ranch with everyone and I loved meeting such interesting people and making them a part of the community I was building. So, we instituted a rule: Guests could stay as long as they like as long as they weren't guests. Everyone who stayed needs to treat the ranch like home, getting water when they need it, finding their own meals, cleaning up after themselves. And everyone helped when there was work to do. On Sunday afternoons, everybody at the ranch would join in a family council meeting to discuss what needed to be done the next week, to divide up meals and chores and such. Occasionally a friend would know a teenager or young adult who wanted to work at the ranch for the summer and we would trade out room and board for help with the animals. That got to be a regular summer event and we had lots of young people who came out year after year to help.

Along with having a house full of people, for the first three months of living there, our house was full of the constant cheep and quack of birds and the living room was lined with large plastic bins full of sawdust and straw. The turkeys, ducks and geese were strong enough not to need a heat lamp, but the chicks still did. That was a problem, since our only electricity came from the red Honda generator that sat on the porch, which we could run occasionally, stretching an extension cord from it to whatever we had to run. When the chicks were young, we ran the pull-start generator at night to fuel the heat lamps, snaking an extension cord through the front door to power them. During the day, I would keep the wood stove extra warm and huddle their plastic boxes around it. I'd used a box cutter to cut the majority of the lids away and hot glued in some chicken wire, so my cats couldn't get in, but the lights and the heat could get through. I loved my little chicks, and, in the evening, I would take the baby ducks and geese to the bathroom, draw a warm bath, and let them swim around. Afterwards I would wrap each one in towels and dry them off before putting them back in their crates. The chicks grew and soon we didn't need the heat lamps anymore.

Moving to Montana had done everything we hoped for and more for my health. My energy was strong. Yes, I still needed a nap most afternoons, but in between resting I could fix fences, hike the trails around our land and (soon) ride horses. I was in love with life. This was everything I had dreamed of, minus not having Dave around that much. But even that had its upside. I loved, at least at first, having it all on my shoulders. I loved the thrill at the end of the day that comes with getting us all through and dealing with all the many emergencies that come with a property like this. Fences came down and the horses got out, a bear broke into the grain bin in the barn and the stallion fell in a narrow but exceptionally deep part of the creek and got stuck. (I had to get neighbors to bring ropes and a truck and help me pull him out.) And every day, no matter what came, I got us through.

Chapter 12

All the Pretty Little Horses

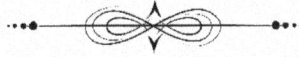

It's four thirty in the afternoon of our first fall at the ranch and I've just returned from picking up my neighbor's kids at school. We'd just met them, these neighbors, but they had an emergency and had asked me if I could cover for them. I made a wide turn at the top of my driveway and drove over the red cattle guard. My tires crunched through half a foot of snow. I hear a loud crack off to my right. As I turned my head to look, a forty-foot pine tree crashed to the ground ten feet from my car.

"Hm," I said. "Look at that."

Then, "Gosh, glad it missed the house!"

The tree did indeed miss the house—by all of five feet. And so did the other one, the one I notice as I gathered up my things and hopped out of the car. A little hard not to notice, this one being one of two huge old pines growing directly through our front porch. It now lay sprawled out across the yard, neatly missing my hammock and coming within two inches of the fence to the horse pasture.

No, our trees aren't rotting, they're just blowing over. We're having a little bit of wind. It happens every time the weather changes. During the last storm, I woke up to hear the dogs frantically barking at the door. I pulled on my coat and boots and stepped outside, to hear a man's voice calling from the top of the driveway, "Yoo Hoo! Hello! It's just me!"

I was puzzled, since I saw no car on the road and in any case, I didn't know any "me's" out here. We'd barely lived here a season. Dave was still in Chicago and my nearest neighbors were half a mile away. "Come on up!" The voice hollered, "Unless you're tired! Or not feeling well! Or you don't want to! Then you don't have to come up, of course! Only if you want to!" By that time, I had reached the top of the driveway, and the voice spotted me.

"Hello, hello! It's just me! Dave!" Alas, no, not my Dave. No, this was Dave, our neighbor to the north. He had apparently hiked over, and he stood in the middle of my driveway in boots and suspenders with a hat pulled down over his ears. He was holding a chainsaw. This was not as odd as it might seem, since he stood behind a very large pine tree which had fallen directly across my driveway.

"I was on my way home from work last night," he called, continually yanking at the chainsaw in a vain attempt to start it, "And I saw you had a tree down, and I thought I better get over here first thing in the morning and get it moved! We don't want you stuck down here; you know! Anything you need, you come and tell us! We just want to help!" And at that point, he finally succeeded in yanking the chainsaw into life, and everything else he said was lost to the roar of the saw.

***

We met our neighbors. One man showed up at our front door with a loaf of fresh baked bread and frightened my mom and Dave's mom (who also joined us for part of that first month) half to death. He looked rough, as people do when they live without running water or electricity and spend their lives working the land. Being city folk, neither of our mothers knew what to make of him: Was he safe? Did they dare invite him in? He and his wife ended up being some of the most interesting and helpful people we met up here. They had homesteaded their property for years, working as forest firefighters during the summer months to earn a little money and raising most of their own food in a small, one room cabin further down the valley. Over the years they taught Dave and I much of what we know about raising animals, gardening at this altitude and butchering our own meat. They were a well-educated couple who listened to the news regularly and kept up on what was going on in the world. But they lived on their own terms.

When we first moved, Dave switched to being a contract worker for his company, a position with less job assurance, but a lot more money. And we had more disposable income than we'd ever had before in our lives. We paid off our credit cards. We bought a new SUV and a horse trailer, and I decorated the house without worry. We added animals to the ranch left and right, never thinking about the feed bills or the vet bills that came with them. I adopted three rescue horses in need of homes and three goats. We bought Dave a Clydesdale, as Dave is a big guy and we figured he would be most comfortable with a bigger horse to ride. And soon our horses arrived from Colorado.

My mom, Karen, Aud and I waited eagerly to get our three horses in. The transport company called us when they were an hour away. We hitched up the new three-horse trailer to our new Suburban and drove down the hill. There was no way we would ask the transport company to drive the last nine miles up that road in their big semi-truck full of horses. We would meet them at a property at the bottom of the hill and drive them up ourselves.

The big truck pulled into the circle drive at the property down the hill. The men calmly lead the horses out. All three of them walked off the truck with no problem. The stallion was as calm as any of them. We loaded them up and took them home.

So now we had seven horses: Three riding horses, three rescues and the Clydesdale which we hoped would become a riding horse in time. Then I brought home three goats, a male and two females. The first day they were there I let them loose, thinking they would enjoy some time in the yard and they all three promptly ran away. I searched for them. I cried. I felt terrible, not having learned yet that most animals need to feel safe in a space before they will stay.

I knew these hills were home to bears and mountain lions, not to mention a sizable wolf pack, and I was pretty sure the goats wouldn't make it on their own. I was wrong. I had about given up on them when, three days after running away, they all three showed up at home, perfectly safe. I rushed to greet them, so happy to see them all and promptly named the male goat, Guard, for his ability to keep the pack of them safe. I named the females Willamina and Annabelle because, well, why not, and they settled into ranch life with the rest of us. They pretty much had the run of the place. It turns out that horse fencing won't keep goats in and nothing we tried to put up on the fly worked either. They climbed over or dug under and took to spending their days on our porch with periodic grazing in the yard. They also ate everything I tried to grow in my garden, all my flowers and all my small trees.

As the summer went on, we soon had a chicken house filled with chickens, a pond full of ducks and geese and a porch full of fat, very large turkeys with stunning feathers and grotesque, blue and purple faces. They, like the goats, quickly abandoned the pen we made for them (it turns out turkeys can fly) and moved onto our back porch where they lined up in front of the two sliding glass doors and stared into the house all day long.

We adopted feral cats from the humane society to live in our barns and do mouse control. We set up rooms in each barn with blankets and beds, scratching posts and feeders. We soon learned that most feral cats don't live very long. They are easy prey to foxes and coyotes among other things. But for however long they survived we fed them and gave them a home. Most of the ones that lived eventually found their way up to the house, discovered the cat door and moved inside, much to the annoyance of our house cats.

At some point, I heard about two donkeys at a rescue who needed a home. We soon added them to the family as well. Oh, and two miniature ponies. Rocky was a red and white paint who was used to roaming the yard at will. In his old house, he would come up to the front porch at dawn every morning where the lady of the house sat to drink her coffee. She would give him a cup of his own and he would stand beside her and drink it as she started her day. Then, every evening, as the husband sat on that same porch drinking an end-of-the-day-beer, Rocky would again come up to the porch and, getting his own beer, hang out with the man as the sun set.

I don't know when I had ever been so happy. I had animals to care for in every corner of the ranch. I had people I enjoyed, living around me. I rode horses every day. My health was the best it had been in years.

***

That first year was magical. As winter came and the snow set in, we had fewer and fewer guests. But with no electric water heaters or running water to the barns, and temperatures which sometimes got down to -30, it took a lot of work to keep the animals fed and watered each day. I trudged through 3 feet of snow to throw out their hay and then had to take a pickaxe to the creek and break the ice down to the running water. As winter went on, I would sometimes have to spend hours sculpting the edges of the creek to allow the horses to safely walk down to the water. In the depth of winter, it would sometimes take two hours to water horses morning and night.

And then there were the goats. Mid-way through the winter, they discovered the dog door and moved into the house. We came home one day to a goat on our bed, one on the back of the couch and one on the kitchen counter, eating a cherry pie. Eventually I had to re-home them, as there was no way to keep them out. I cried to see them go.

That first winter I was out fixing fences one day in February in temperatures below -10 degrees and I stepped wrong. I plunged through the ice and right into the deepest part of the creek. As I fought my way out of the creek, weighed down by fencing tools of all sorts, the water was already turning to ice inside my clothes. I knew I had to get out of the cold now and I dropped what I was carrying and stumbled towards the house. As I tripped up the steps to the back deck, I spotted the sauna and knew that was the quickest way to get warm. I turned on the propane heater full blast and stripped off my clothes, dropping them in the snow between the sauna and my bedroom door. The sauna heated up fast and I sat on its wooden bench breathing a sigh of relief as the ice fell away and the heat returned to my limbs.

***

My mom had spent the first summer with us and loved the whole adventure. She wanted to come back every summer and we began talking about building up the little cabin on the Middle Twenty so she could have a place of her own. No electricity or running water and only an outhouse for a bathroom, but she was game to give it a try. She had never done anything like this before but was getting ready to transition from being a full-time church pastor to a sort of semi-retirement where she would write, lead workshops, and fill in at local churches. She wanted to live a contemplative life in a simple location where she could focus on her writing and her prayer. Not for the whole year, but for a few months every summer. And she wanted to be closer to her kids as, at least for my sister and brother, her first grandkids began to be born. We reached out to my friend, Curry, from my Colorado days, and asked him to come spend the summer with us and help us build the cabin my mother would live in. He agreed.

On our first Memorial Day weekend at the ranch, we invited everyone we knew to come for a cabin raising. With 24 people sleeping crashed out on every corner of the house we felled trees, scraped off the bark and turned the little half cabin into a full-fledged cabin with a large downstairs and an upstairs loft. In one weekend, we got the walls up and the structure built, and Curry stayed on to finish the rest. By the end of the summer, we had a large downstairs room and an upstairs, lofted bedroom, which my mom would live in every summer for the next twenty years.

***

A year into our Montana life I spent two months sleeping in the barn desperately trying to be present for the births of my two mares. Mares have a great deal of control over when they give birth. They typically go eleven months but can go ten or even thirteen. If they are not comfortable with their situation, they can start the process then stop it and wait for a better time. They can, and do, put it off for weeks or months if they do not feel safe in

116

their given situations. And one of the things that makes a mare not feel safe is the presence of people.

Mares give birth alone. They leave the herd and find a quiet spot and do the whole process by themselves. Not that there is much to the process. The birth rarely takes more than half an hour from start to finish and can easily take as little as five minutes total. Assuming nothing goes wrong, a horse's birth is sudden and quick. It is a common story among horse owners that you sleep in the barn every night for a month, only to go back to the house for a cup of coffee one morning and find the foal fully born when you return. But these two mares were both experienced broodmares and unusually people oriented. Though I spent a month sleeping in the barn in the fear that the foals would come early, in the end they were both born right on time with me right there. There were no problems with either birth, so I didn't need to call the vet and only had him come out after each birth to do a New Foal Checkup. The morning after the first birth I called the people we had bought these horses from in Colorado. We had stayed in touch, and I'd spent a lot of time on the phone, learning from them, as the birthing times neared. I was beside myself with news about the black, curly headed, moose-faced baby that had just been born. They shared my excitement. "Is he beautiful???" they asked.

I paused just a little too long. He was wonderful. But well... actually, he looked a great deal like a moose. (I was later to learn that most Rocky Mountain Horses looked awkward and moose-like at birth.) I rushed to answer. "I'm sure he has a great personality!"

The births were a revelation to me. Never had I seen anything like them. The quiet mother, waiting, waiting. The weeks of nothing and then suddenly, a baby, emerging from the mother's body whole and alive. I was in love.

I was in love, not only with the foals themselves, but with the whole process of having foals. I loved it so much that when a few months later the couple from Post Rock Ranch called me up and asked if I wanted to buy out their business, I jumped at the chance. They wanted to retire and didn't want to scatter their life's work to the winds. They would sell us seven mares and their primary stallion, and they would finance the purchase themselves. Dave agreed. It was a great opportunity for me to do something I loved and Rocky Mountain Horses were selling for $10,000 - $20,000 a piece at that time.

Soon we were birthing eight babies per year and breeding both our mares and mares belonging to other people. We had two stallions. Within a couple of years, we had thirty horses and were selling a few each season.

Chapter 13

My Beloved Rajah

Rajah, my German Shepherd, stood by my side while we ran a horse ranch together. He led the way on trail rides, never letting a horse and rider leave the barn without him. He protected me on camping trips and on my many late-night wanderings around the ranch. He stood by my side day and night, guarding all that was mine. We were partners, running the ranch together. Everyone loved him. He quickly befriended everyone he met. He was a rarity among German Shepherds in that he was not intimidating even to those who were normally leery of dogs. Not unless he wanted to be, that is. He was so friendly and so *happy* all the time that it was hard to remember his big teeth and police dog looks unless he wanted you to see him that way. He made everybody laugh and bonded with special friends everywhere he went. Kids loved him, adults loved him. And he spread his love liberally among them all.

But his bond to me was something else again. No matter who he was buttering up at any given moment, Rajah always kept one eye on me. He was my constant companion, and I was his world.

Have you ever been loved like that by a dog? It is one of the greatest gifts this life has to give. This creature, so noble and so strong, chooses you to worship, live for, love. He chooses you to serve. And his service is absolute.

With Rajah, I always felt like a queen with a wise counselor by my side. When he wasn't being a goof, he was so serious, so watchful and ready. He watched my world. And he always stood by to serve and protect.

Rajah wasn't our only dog. While we were in Chicago, we had gotten a second dog as a buddy for him. Maya was a Rottweiler/boxer mix. From day one, Maya, a fun loving but much more serious dog than Rajah, was Rajah's best friend. They adored each other and were inseparable. And then we had our great Pyrenees, Cirrus, whom we had inherited from a neighbor who moved onto our mountain then decided not to stay. She was an awesome dog whose instincts led her to spend her nights guarding the ranch and all its animals from the many predators who roam these hills. She adored people but knew that her priority was the animals she was born to protect.

It has always been a priority for me that my animals have as free and natural a life as I can give them. Our birds free-range over sixty acres (though with all that room, why their location of choice always ends up being our nice wooden deck, I don't know.) Our horses live in large pastures with creeks, fields, and wooded hills.

We have had dogs visit who threatened the birds or other animals. Most at least have to be taught to leave such creatures alone. But Rajah never did. He knew what was mine. He always had. He lived to protect that which I had claimed. That was who he was. I trusted him with my life. I trusted him with my soul. Then, one day, something changed.

***

As Rajah reached ten years of age, old for a German Shepherd, he took on some new behaviors. Nothing sudden or overt. Annoying, a little disturbing, but mostly easy to ignore. My horse breeding business was booming, taking off much more quickly than I expected. My health was on the downswing. I was struggling to keep up. The ranch was wonderful but hard; feeding, fencing, animals that always needed something. I worked all day when I could and held things together by a shoestring. I loved my life, but it was exhausting, and it took everything I had.

So, there were changes. We'd recently started joking that in his old age Rajah had "accessed his inner shepherd." He's started frantically throwing himself into herding. The problem was, he wasn't very good at it. Likely as not, he sent the animals right back at me or got them running in completely the wrong direction. And once they ran, he chased even more frantically, barking and barking. Once he got going, he was very hard to stop.

At first, Rajah's herding behavior was just a mixture of exasperating and endearing. He wanted so much to help; I could hardly hold it against him. But he was annoying, and at times even dangerous. My first ride on a young horse is not the best time for a frantic, barking dog to be doing laps around its legs. And I didn't like the way he became obsessed with chasing the ones that ran. He seemed to grow a violent side that I had never seen before. And it took yelling over and over to snap him out of it, get his attention and convince him to quit.

But in other moments Rajah was Rajah, faithful and dependable forever. And I had been so busy struggling every day to make headway on the endless list of things I had to do before winter settled in. I registered the change, but I never really took the time to stop and think about it.

Rajah especially loved to torment the goats and my half-grown lamb, whom I had raised from a baby. We stopped him when we could, but we were getting used to his chasing and sometimes we just didn't have time to deal with it.

The lamb, and sometimes the goats, followed me about my work all day, even going on hikes with me or following me up the trail when I rode my horses around these mountains. I loved my goats; they made me laugh. And I especially loved my lamb. I called him Lamie. I had raised him in the house for two months, dressing him in diapers and onesies, and then, reluctantly, as he grew, I moved him to a stall in the goat pasture. Every morning, I would go out and get him so that he could spend the day with me. When I let him out of his pen, he would race joyfully down the hill beside me. In his excitement, unable to contain his joy, he would kick up his hind legs so far that he flipped himself over backwards, then landed and did it all again. He made me laugh, and I loved the feel of his soft wool as I went about my tasks, often resting my hand on his head or scratching him behind the ears.

Dave loved Lamie too, as did my neighbors who sometimes worked for me. Everyone loved him. But his love was especially and mostly for me. He followed me everywhere and was never happier than when he was by my side.

We all saw Rajah tormenting Lamie. In his sudden obsession with herding, he would force Lamie to run around the yard, herding him this way and that until I scolded him and made him stop. That would give Lamie a break until I got distracted and Rajah started up again.

The day things changed was a Saturday in spring. I was outside, moving hay around the ranch. The goats and Lamie were racing around the yard and Rajah was racing around them, barking, as usual.

My neighbor was at the ranch that day. I looked over to see him running up the driveway from the barn, calling frantically, but what he said didn't make any sense. "Christie," he shouted, "Rajah just killed Lamie!"

I stared at him. Was Lamie actually dead? And surely, he didn't mean Rajah. Was a neighbor's dog around? Had some other dog killed my lamb? My neighbor shouted, "Lamie's still alive but he's killed him. There's no way he's going to survive. Rajah just ripped out his throat!"

I stared behind him. Rajah was racing happily up the driveway towards us. He had blood on his face and mouth.

But I was sure there was a mistake. Until my neighbor spoke again.

"I saw Rajah tormenting Lamie like he sometimes does, and I was going down there to tell him to cut it out. Then I saw Rajah lunge for Lamie's throat. He ripped it out. I saw the blood spray. There's no way Lamie is going to live."

Just then Rajah reached me. "Go in your crate," I told him, still trying to get my mind around what my neighbor had said. Rajah ran straight inside, directly to his crate. I closed the door and left him there. On the way through the house, it hit me that this was really happening. I called to Dave, and yelled (a little hysterically), "Dave, Rajah just killed Lamie!"

122

"What??" Dave shouted.

"Rajah just killed Lamie! He ripped out his throat! He's not dead yet, but he's going to die!"

Dave's voice was as shocked as mine. "Oh my God!" He said. A pause, then, "I'll be right out!"

I ran to Lamie, my mind still confused, still unable to understand how this had happened. Was my neighbor exaggerating? Was Lamie really that badly hurt? Surely not. Maybe it was just a scratch. Maybe it was not so bad.

But the soft, thick wool around Lamie's throat was soaked in blood. There was a pool under his head and more poured out as I watched. Lamie, looking dazed, lay on his side, breathing raggedly. I dropped to my knees in front of him. There was no way he was going to live. My neighbor was there, telling me again what had happened, as shocked as I was. "Any other dog," he said. "I'd expect this of any other dog, but not Rajah."

I didn't know what to do. I knew Lamie was suffering, and we had to put him down. "I have to tell Dave to get his gun," I started to stumble towards the house. But the minute I stood, Lamie lurched to his feet, trying to follow. He staggered three steps and fell. My mind cleared a little and I knew I couldn't leave him. I asked my neighbor to go for the gun. I dropped down next to my lamb.

Dave arrived, gun in hand. I kissed Lamie's beautiful white nose and lurched up and stumbled a few feet away. "Christie, you need to go over there," my neighbor said, pointing behind Dave, "If he's gonna shoot in that direction, you can't stand there..."

I moved away. I heard the crack of the gun, and my tears began to fall. Eventually Dave came up behind me, gently turned me towards him and wrapped his arms around me. I choked out, "Is he dead?" And he said, "Yes," and let me cry.

I went inside and walked up to Rajah's crate. I looked him in the eyes and yelled, "How could you? How could you kill my Lamie? How could you do a thing like that?" I was sobbing too hard to say more, so I threw a blanket over his crate. I didn't want to see him anymore. I went out and closed the door. I sat in the living room and cried. I called my mother and my best friend. Dave took me to dinner to get me away from the ranch for a while. We left Rajah in his crate.

Being in his crate was normal for Rajah and not necessarily a punishment. He loved his crate. It was big enough for him to comfortably lay out and turn around in. It sat beside my bed, in my bedroom, and had in every house we had slept in since Rajah came to live with me. He ate meals in his crate. He got treats in his crate. When he was tired or stressed, he went to his crate and curled up on his soft pillow with his favorite blanket and soothed the worries of the day. But we also used it as punishment those few times he got into trouble. We would put him in there and I would leave, separating him from me. This allows for the separation, which is his punishment, but also leaves him with the comfort of his familiar surroundings.

But this was different. For two days, we kept Rajah locked in his crate except for leashed walks in the yard to do his business. When I saw him, I never smiled at him, never gave him any love. I looked him in the eye and said, "What you did is not acceptable. I can't talk to you about it yet." And then I refused to acknowledge him at all. I left the blanket over his crate so that he could not see me, even though I still slept just two feet away in my own bed.

Rajah was devastated. He was terrified. He looked at me desperately every time I approached, ears pulled back, shaking violently, crying horrible, desperate cries deep in his throat. I was his world and I had taken myself away from him completely.

For two days, I worked around the ranch with a lump in my stomach and tears in my eyes, working hard enough that I didn't have time to stop and think about the way Rajah looked at me, the desperate shaking, the dreadful, heartbreaking noise he made. Two nights I sat up, unable to sleep, terrified that somehow Rajah would die that night, never knowing that I still loved him. I paced the house all night, telling myself that I couldn't let up. Rajah had to know—had to never forget—that this was not something he could ever do again.

Dogs don't process events the same way people do. I know that. But I also know that a devastating reaction to what he did would make an impression. I had to let him know this wasn't okay. It might mean the difference between him being a safe dog and a dangerous one.

Monday morning, I went to him. I sat in front of him and told him to look me in the eye. I said, "You are my Rajah and what you did hurt me. I never thought that you could do such a thing. I never thought you would let me down, betray me like that. I don't know what to do about it. I don't know why you did it. But we will figure those things out together. You are my Rajah and I still love you. You will still be mine until the day that you die. But things are going to be different for a while." I put on his leash, and we went out to do our morning chores.

The vet ran tests to see if she could find something wrong with Rajah to explain what had happened. Maybe he had been in pain lately. Maybe this was why he'd changed. The tests were inconclusive. Yes, he had some pain. Some arthritis in his joints. But he never showed it. So, we had no way to judge how bad it was. Was it bad enough to push him to lose himself to his primal drives this completely? We found indication that he'd broken his leg once—something we had never known about. There is nothing so stoic as a German Shepherd on the job. So, it was certainly possible that he was in pain—lots of pain—and we didn't know it. We started him on pain meds just in case.

It was also possible that he was jealous of Lamie, the time I spent with him. Or maybe he was becoming confused in his old age and his instincts to herd and to hunt were mixing, overriding his normal behavior. The truth was we didn't know what was wrong or why it had happened. And we didn't know what to do.

My Rajah-B, the truest companion of my life, he who had barely seen a leash since we moved to Montana, who ran free everywhere he went; was he to be chained now, forever? At what point, should I trust him again? At what point, would I be able to say, "Ok, now we know he would never do that again." Was he dangerous to people now? Was I to watch him every minute? I felt like I had lost my Rajah and yet he was still there.

And that's the thing, isn't it? He was still there. He deserved more from me than this. He had given me all his life, all his heart and all his soul. He'd been the perfect dog and now I felt betrayed.

After all that he had given me, didn't he deserve to know that in my heart he was still my perfect dog? Didn't he deserve, somehow, for me to say, "You are all I could have asked for," and to keep on loving him with the same devotion I had always had before?

So how would I do that and still keep my animals safe? How would I accept this change and not let that diminish all that Rajah was? I was tired. I missed my Lamie. I hurt at the prospect of taking my Rajah's freedom away.

Rajah was in his crate, asleep, exhausted after our first day back together. I soaked in a bath while Dave read a book to me. Later, I cooked an artichoke and poured myself a glass of wine. Somehow, I had to find a way to be faithful to Rajah, whatever might come. He deserved that from me. He deserved the love I had always given him, the pride I'd always had in him. He deserved to feel me say every day, "You are my perfect dog." Even if, just that once, he wasn't.

Shortly after that Rajah's herding behavior eased, going back to normal levels. I was always hyper aware of how he was feeling and watched him for signs he needed to slow down or rest or simply take a time out and collect himself. But he went back to normal and stayed that way, never again showing any signs of aggression. He was once again my perfect dog, and I spent the rest of his life making sure he knew it.

CHAPTER 14

Forty-Six Pregnant Lamas

Five years into our Montana adventure I said to Dave, "I'd like to have some goats again. For milk. Maybe meat. I hear they are very good at weed control." We had stopped using the dog door as our dogs became older and less inclined to go outside without us. I missed Guard, Annabelle, and Willamina. It seemed like time to try again.

"I'd be behind getting a few goats for those things," he agreed. A week later I came home with seven goats, six of them pregnant. Within six months we had 14 goats. What we didn't have was a pen that could keep them in. Goat fencing needs to be strong and well-built, with a special type of wire buried a foot underground. What we had wasn't up to par. So, these goats, like our first crew, lived where they pleased. Mostly that ended up being our front porch and it was not uncommon to see a goat, nose pushed against the living room window, staring in at us longingly. They clearly thought that they had gotten the rotten end of the deal in living outside and in the goat barn. The house was their dearest desire.

And while goats may well eat weeds, I quickly found out that they eat them only AFTER they have eaten all the flowers, decorative vines and small trees within their reach—and a wide reach it is, since they can get over or under any fence and clearly preferred standing on the hood of our car to standing in the pasture we painstakingly prepared for them.

This did not go over well with Dave. But what could we do? Dave suggested having roast goat, but we compromised by always parking the car in the garage. The goats weren't *that* in the way, and besides, they made me laugh. Every morning when I opened my eyes, they would be standing there at my bedroom window, their noses pushed against the glass, staring at me.

And they followed me around the ranch all day, entertaining themselves by stealing my dog's Frisbee and daring him to brave their horns and get it back. When it rained, they'd all huddle on the porch and I had to step over the goats every time I went outside.

Dave took it all in with a worried expression. He didn't want to squash my joy but as the years passed, he was struggling with the chaos and the number of animals was starting to worry him.

* * *

I'd been breeding horses for over five years and at eight foals per year I had quickly become an expert at the job. And I loved baby animals of all kinds—birds, goats, sheep, and horses. I wanted to pour love into every baby I saw. So, one day when I got a call from a rescue group in town I listened eagerly as they told me they had forty-six pregnant lamas in need of an immediate home. Another rescue had folded, after doing an inadequate job of keeping the males and females apart. They needed an experienced rancher to get the lamas through the many births and give them a home while the rescue sorted them out and began the long process of adopting them out to permanent homes. I was ecstatic. Who *wouldn't* want forty-six pregnant lamas? *Was there anything better than this?*

I rushed around to make room for them all, and the rescue loaded them into trucks and started up our road. They got about halfway up the hill before they turned around. They called me from the bottom. "There is no way we are getting our trucks up that road. We will have to take the lamas to somebody else." I was heartbroken, and maybe, just slightly relieved. I still regret not having those lamas. (*Can you think of anything more beautiful than all those tiny lama babies?*) But I also know that by then I was pushing the limits of my health once again and barely holding on.

When I look back now, many years on from the lama decision, I see that whole episode as an apt metaphor for how I lived my life back then: Jumping into the things I loved with both feet, never hesitating, throwing my arms open wide and taking it all on. The forty-six pregnant lamas have become a symbol to me of my love of life and my willingness to embrace every opportunity that came my way. But also, it whispers of the flip side of that willingness: Embracing challenges that would extract great costs from us without weighing whether we could pay those costs.

And Dave, it must be said, breathed a major sigh of relief when the lamas fell through. He enjoyed the animals in his way but was much more aware than I was of the damage I was doing to my body by constantly taking in all these lives which relied on me so completely. It was just after the lamas that he asked for an agreement between us. From then on, we needed to both agree before either of us brought home any new lives. No more leaving to buy one goat and returning with fourteen. No more lamas, pregnant or otherwise, unless we had talked it through first. And with that rule, our lives began, if only in a small way, to stabilize. Because all those lives filled my heart, but they also filled my days, my nights and my everything in between. And because, as Dave realized long before I ever did, there came a cost with every life. Not just the financial cost or the physical work each life took. But the emotional toll. Because animals died. Even if they lived a full, long life, eventually, and long before us, they died. And every death ripped us apart anew.

***

We loved this life. When we lived in Chicago, I spent hundreds of dollars per month on clothes and make-up and hair styles. Now, if my hair needed cutting, I just grabbed a pair of scissors and whacked it off myself. And I put on make-up, maybe four times a year. Our lives were very different, and we are learning a whole new set of skills. We were also learning a whole new way of looking at the world and being forced to come to terms with things that modern life no longer prepares most Americans to face. Things like death.

Farm life—ranch life—is full of death. I didn't know this, when we first drove our blue jeep Cherokee up this bumpy mountain road and onto the 60-

acre property which was to become the center of our lives. Since I left Chicago, it has been an on-going struggle for me to understand, to accept, and to live with death.

Once upon a time, most Americans knew what I was just beginning to learn. Many of us were farmers and even those that weren't had some relationship to animals, both as food and as workers that modern people have forgotten all about. Most people had the experience of knowing personally at least some of the animals that ended up on their table at dinner time. In days past, people were required from time to time to kill a living creature for food. To deal with this, some people often came to see animals as a means to an end and not as sacred individuals. I was still struggling to find a different way to relate to my animals. I wanted to retain my love of each individual and yet still be able to let them go when it was time. I never expected it to be this hard.

I grew up a city girl. Suburban really, with some city thrown in here and there. Nobody I knew lived on a farm or a ranch. What I have done is unique in my family and among my friends. I've had to learn it all from scratch.

The first time one of my chickens died, I cried like a baby. But we've had hundreds of chickens since, and dozens upon dozens of ducks, geese, turkeys, and such. And birds die easily. If it's not a brave coyote who slips through our defenses, then it's a horse's hoof stomping down on the oblivious bird when it wanders its way into a stall. One winter we had a "house duck" for three months when one of our ducks broke its leg. We brought it in and cared for it, drawing it a bath every night and endlessly cleaning up its poop. But it eventually died from its injuries and there was nothing we could do. The first time my rabbits had babies, I rushed them all inside and struggled for three days to feed them with bottles and formula, only to find out, after half of them were dead, that what I believed was the abandonment of the mother was actually normal. Mother rabbits only come to their litter once a day. They would have been fine if I'd just left them alone. I felt sick with guilt.

I would never make it in this life if I continued to be as hurt by each death as I was by those first few. How could I teach myself not to be so hurt by every death, while still caring personally about each life?

That question became more important when we decided to begin raising our own meat. Unable to support the kind of torture most commercial feed animals have to live through, we resolved not to buy commercial meat again. The first year we lived at the ranch we had a vague desire to raise our own meat and we got a bunch of chickens. But we weren't ready for the reality of the killing, and we just ended up with 40 pet chickens. Since then, we have spent a lot of time soul searching on this issue, and we finally came to a place where we were able, usually, to kill the animals we raised to eat.

On this mountain, there is a couple, both highly educated, able to hold their own in any modern city if they choose, who left normal city life to live a more independent life in nature. Their names are Bob and Dynah and they have taught us a lot about living up here. This couple chooses to spend their days making their way by their own two hands and living in a way they feel they can ethically justify. As such, they give up money and scrape by on very little. They have no generator (and thus, no electricity), no running water, and they live in a small, one room cabin they built for themselves.

For financial and ethical reasons, this couple raises all their own food. Being Montana that means mostly meat, as the growing season is short, and their garden produces only so much.

They clearly love their animals and most of their creatures approach them with trust. In the fall, they do their own butchering. We asked them if they had trouble with the butchering. I didn't know if I would be capable of killing an animal I love. If I raised my own animals, I said, I would have to take them to a butcher to be killed.

They told me they hate butchering season. It is their hardest time of the year. But they believe it is their obligation to do the butchering themselves. Putting the animal in a trailer, driving it into town and giving it to a stranger

131

creates too much trauma for the animal. They feel they have no right to make the animal's death that difficult just to save the humans' sensibilities. It is their responsibility to give the animals a good death as well as a good life.

When it's time for butchering, they prepare the animal's favorite meal. They sit with the animal and thank it. Then they shoot it through the head.

That sounds awful, doesn't it? Violent and abrasive. But the animal is dead before it knows that anything is going to happen. For the human, it's traumatic, but the animal experiences none of that. For the animal, this is a very peaceful death.

That's the goal: To give my animals the best, happiest, most natural life I can, and then to make their deaths as quick and painless as possible. That's the goal, but the reality is proving much more difficult to live with.

The creator of this universe made the world such that death is not only unavoidable; it is necessary for the continuance of life. So, if I believe that the creator of the universe is good, shouldn't this mean that death is also good? Surely the universe was not created to revolve around an evil process.

Surely this is true. But how I am to accept it, I have no idea.

When Lamie died, after we had cried about it, Dave took his body and butchered it. It was understood between us that when this kind of thing happened, we would butcher and eat the lost animal. My city-bred background, so insulated from death, wanted to laugh at the absurdity of that. The city part of me finds this kind of sentiment appropriate to a cannibal or a serial killer. How can you grieve a friend and then say, "Oh well," and serve him up with a good cream sauce? But I will not deny my lamb his right to take his place in nature's version of eternal life, in the ultimate sacrifice of giving his life so that others may live. So now that he is dead, his body becomes food. He becomes the very stuff of life. I believe in that; I even think it's sacred. But I have to admit, I didn't eat much the night he graced our table. I just couldn't do it.

My head approves of this approach to life. But my heart, my heart is not there yet. I know death is a sacred process which takes us on to our next adventure. I know we are all meat, each meant to take our place, eventually, as the food that feeds the world. I believe those things. Yet it hurts. No matter what my head reasons, losing an animal I love always hurts.

***

I killed a horse today. Held a 45 to her skull and shot her through the head. She fell so fast I hardly took in that she was dead, but there was the hole in her head as proof, shooting out blood like a broken pipe, thick and red and pulsing. She was dead before she had time to notice the gun.

I had expected the killing part to be harder than it was, that somehow the gun would be heavy, the trigger would take strength to pull. I thought I'd have to hold her head and struggle to keep her still. But I didn't. The gun was light in my hand. The trigger was easy to pull. I squeezed and it was done. She pitched sideways as her legs collapsed and hit the ground while I was still standing there, expecting to have something more to do.

Earlier that day I had talked to her before loading her into the trailer, and again after unloading her, and before walking her into the woods. She struggled to walk those first few steps, hobbling on legs that shook in place with pain. I stood for a minute, my face resting against her forehead and called her, "Dear child," in a quiet, gentle voice. I told her it was almost over. She had only a little way to go. "I just need you to walk a few more steps and then I'll take care of everything. That's all you need to do. Come baby-doll. Come my dear one. A few more steps. That's all."

She followed me, trusting, into the woods, no longer hesitating despite the pain in her legs. She walked willingly through the trees, over the downed branches and the undergrowth. When we reached the place that I had chosen, I stood for a minute and thanked her again, told her she was done, and the pain would be over soon. It was like she'd been in a trance, these last few

133

hours, her big eyes fixed on me, calm and trusting. Trusting me to do what needed to be done.

I floundered for a moment, looking for the right words, the right ritual to send her on her way. I sensed immediately that her trance began to slip. Her eyes left my face, and she began to look around. She shifted uneasily and lifted her head. In a second of clarity, I saw that the ritual, the something more, was something I needed. She didn't need it. She needed me to act quickly and decisively and do what had to be done. She needed me to continue with confidence while she still rested in her trust in me before my hesitation and emotions brought her back to fear.

I stopped talking and lifted the gun. I pulled the trigger, just like that. No stopping to reposition. No careful evaluating of the angle or position of my arm. Before she could register what I was doing, I pulled the trigger, and she was down.

I had thought out the method, picked out the place, been talking to Stormy for weeks, asking her to tell me when it was time for her to go. I had known for most of a year that her time was coming soon. She was thirty-five years old and had been in poor health for a couple of years now. Stormy was in pain. She had rallied and recovered many times. It was clear to me that she would not recover this time. My horse, the dear, quiet girl with the long face and sleek black body, who never refused a person's request and ruled the other horses without a second thought, was at the end of the life she was meant to live. For years, she graced my pastures, raised my weanling foals, and ate the food that I provided. Now she couldn't walk without pain. She had stopped leaving the barn to find food. She wouldn't graze, she was hardly willing to walk twenty feet to drink water anymore. In the wild she would have been left behind long ago, taken down by an animal that was younger, stronger, at the beginning of its time to live. But this old girl was not in the wild. She was in my care. She had long ago made the deal with my kind that she would obey and serve, and that we, in return, would provide for her that which she needed but could not provide for herself. And today the thing she needed but could not provide for herself was death.

I thought this would feel beautiful to me, that the killing itself would be hard, but that once her spirit was gone, I would be at peace to let her body take its place in the circle of life. But she did not look at peace in the wilderness, she did not look like a natural part of the beauty of the land. She looked like a beautiful body that I had loved, brushed, cared for, lying twisted in the dirt. No hiker, stumbling into our thicket in the woods, would find her a peaceful sight and be comforted by the beauty of her body's journey as it returned to the earth. She looked dead. There was a hole in her head and blood pooled beneath her face and gushed out of the hole as though it would never stop. And soon the bear would come and the coyotes and the wolves, maybe a mountain lion or two, and the flies and the worms, and none of this would be the graceful, gentle merging with nature that I imagined it to be.

The fact is, there is nothing graceful about a bullet in the head.

Nobody taught me how to do this kind of thing. Killing, in the city, the world from which I came, is a cruel thing, evil, to be shunned at all costs. Nobody told me that sometimes killing is a kindness, and nobody told me that even so, the killing itself is never kind.

Who, in my city world, prepared me for dealing out death? Who told me that being responsible for the lives in my care would eventually mean arranging for their deaths? Who warned me that a gun, bought for protection, would be used to kill a thing I loved because it was my job to help her when her suffering became too much?

That morning, she had stared at me when I came into her stall. Her big eyes, calm and deep, looked right into me. She hadn't moved even a step in two days, and I knew it was time. So, I did the thing that was mine to do. I slipped the halter over her head and whispered to her quietly while I stroked her neck and scratched her ears. Then I led her to a trailer and drove her to the woods. I left her body for the wolves and bears to eat, and I went home and cleaned my gun.

CHAPTER 15

Running Full Speed

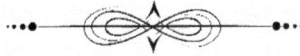

I Loved our life at the ranch, despite the regular heartbreak that went along with it. I grabbed what energy I had with both hands. Within eight years we had thirty horses. Fourteen goats. Twenty-Eight Chickens, thirteen turkeys, seven ducks and Nine geese. We also had solar panels and a battery bank plus a generator to provide electricity for the house. For the first time, we could flip a switch at night and fill the house with light. But we still heated with a wood stove, meaning wood had to be brought in and the house cleaned from the perpetual layer of grimy dust that the wood smoke left behind. Our wood stove is unusual and something we have always loved about this home. It is a giant contraption taken from an old steam engine and it is big enough for a medium-sized person to climb into. It fits two-foot logs and, when stocked full, will heat the house for 24 hours without needing to be refilled. The downside of this is that it is leaky and not airtight and this exacerbates the problem of wood stoves—mainly that they cause the house to be far dirtier than other types of heat. And I liked the house clean. If you don't dust every day, you quickly get a film of tacky black dust over everything.

***

And so, the years moved on. I pushed myself every day to get done some fraction of the constant work that the ranch required. After the first couple of years, Dave spent most of his time at the ranch with only occasional forays back to Chicago. He got an office in town and drove to Missoula most days for work, since we didn't have an internet solution good enough to allow him to work from home. He had a full-time job, whether he was working in

Montana or in Chicago. The ranch was my job. I was the rancher, and he was the rancher's husband.

There was so much I wanted to do in this new life, and I tried to do it all. I taught riding lessons, trained horses, and offered trail rides to small groups. I hired out to host birthday parties and family BBQs and occasionally had groups come stay for a week of riding, lessons, and good food. We offered a very casual experience, cots set up in the living room or a bed in the loft, but for those who wanted that kind of personal experience it was a wonderful adventure. I rode every day. All of my broodmares were excellent riding horses and so I had eight horses I could trust with any rider. My business was booming, and I loved every minute of it.

Eventually, of course, this level of activity took its toll. Eight years after moving to Montana, I was in pain again, fighting exhaustion and becoming less and less able to do the work of the ranch myself. Twice, while out riding, I passed out on the back of my horse and this breed proved its worth when the mare I was riding quietly walked me home, standing at the front porch with me unconscious across her back until someone noticed and came to help. I began to have more trouble handling the stallions and increasingly I would find myself down at the barn, unable to continue, and have to lay down on the hay and sleep until I was strong enough to make the short walk from the barn back to the house. In the summer this was just a nuisance, but in the winter, it got dangerous. Dave took to watching my movements closely so that he could come looking for me if I didn't return when expected. And increasingly, on bad days, I didn't feel safe going outside on my own.

* * *

A bad day with CFS/ME is a lot like that day when you have the flu, just after the throwing up stage has passed when you find yourself so weak that just walking down the hallway is exhausting. When the fatigue gets that bad, brain fog becomes a problem, making it difficult to think clearly or speak normally. I stumbled over words. I stuttered through every thought. During these times, it became like pulling teeth to have even simple conversations. My hands would shake after just a little exertion, and I developed twitches in my face that came out when I was tired. And as time went on at the ranch, I was always tired.

Then, of course, there is the pain, muscles, and joints. Sometimes an ache and sometimes a screaming, stabbing attack. This wasn't arthritis pain. This pain came from extreme exhaustion.

My first major crash (bad enough to require months of bed rest) happened about five years into our Montana adventure. After that, life was a constant cycle of building up my strength, then going too far and crashing again, then months of recovery only to repeat the whole process. I always got hopeful when the cycle turned up again and my strength increased. I always threw myself into all the things I dreamed of doing, somehow not realizing that these improvements would not last. But, as had been the case when I was younger, each crash left me a little less recovered than the time before, and soon, even on good days, I was struggling just to keep up with the basic care and feeding the animals required to stay alive. Not that the basics were any small thing. Feeding and watering thirty horses was a full-time job.

By February of each year this was a two-hour process twice a day and was far more than I could manage. We had to hire a neighbor to help. We had paid off many of our debts when we first moved to Montana but even with Dave's income, we were beginning to fill up our credit cards again. The horse business earned us some money, but never as much as we spent on it, and even with insurance, my medical expenses were high. We were back to living paycheck to paycheck most months, just trying to keep afloat. Still, I couldn't run the ranch alone anymore so more and more often we pulled out our credit cards and put the problem off for another day.

* * *

Around this time the economy took a drastic downward turn. It was January when Dave got the call. He was being laid off, starting the next day.

Him being a contractor, they could do this with no severance package or notice. Suddenly, with one day's warning, we found ourselves with no income of any kind. The horses weren't selling because horse sales always slow down in winter and because the crash in the economy was affecting my business too. Suddenly there were no buyers lining up to buy our horses. Suddenly we had thirty horses and no sales in sight.

Dave was out of work for six months. We lived on credit cards and loans from family and friends. We took out loans from a local bank. Young horses which would have sold for $5000 before the crash I was now selling for $500 just to get us free of the regular farrier and vet expenses. Adult horses still sold for a bit more but now they were closer to $3000 rather than the $10,000 we used to get. So, our income from the business dropped drastically but our expenses did not. Horses still needed their hooves trimmed. They needed to be wormed and fed and to have regular vet visits. Add to that the fact that my health was crashing at this time as well, and now I could no longer train my own horses. Hiring a trainer to train a young horse costs at least $1500, sometimes twice that. Given that, at that time, each horse cost about $500 to feed each year, and a horse wasn't ridable until it was at least three years old, each horse cost a minimum of $4000 to raise. In short, we were no longer breaking even on the horses. More and more of my business expenses went on credit cards and between that and Dave being out of work it wasn't long before our credit cards were maxed out again.

***

I had four nieces now and two of them lived nearby, in Missoula. I knew from the start that I would not have kids of my own and I poured myself into my nieces without hesitation. I'd been present at the birth of both of my Missoula nieces and spent a lot of my time babysitting them. It was important to me that I be a central part of their lives. I was also involved with my brother's kids, but they were 1700 miles away in St. Louis and I only saw them once a year, so I didn't know them quite as well.

My niece, Lucy, the oldest of my two local nieces, loved horses. I took her riding every chance I got, sitting with me in the saddle, clinging to me as I steered the horse. One afternoon, when she was three years old, I took her on a horseback ride up into the woods behind our house. Her father rode beside us on another of my horses. She laughed and chattered away, shouting, "Faster! Faster!" and throwing up her hands in delight.

I probably shouldn't have been cantering. Lucy's "Faster! Faster!" was so full of delight that I couldn't resist. And I was an accomplished rider. I rarely lost my seat. But here we were, loping along, and the horse, possibly made ungainly and off balance by her pregnancy, tripped. She hit a rock or stepped in a hole. Her knees hit the ground and Lucy and I flew over her head.

I've asked myself a million times since that day: Was it irresponsible to canter with a child in my arms? Should I not have asked a pregnant mare to run? But we were doing a very slow canter—one of those that is barely as fast as a trot. And I rode my pregnant mares all the time. Horses trip. It happens. I wouldn't have lost my seat if it weren't that at the very moment the horse tripped, Lucy lunged to the side, shouting, "Look at that!" and I had to lunge halfway out of the saddle to keep her in my arms. Off balance and already half out of my seat, I had no chance of staying in the saddle when the horse went down.

By the time her father knew something was wrong, we were already on the ground. I had held fast to Lucy, twisting in midair so that I would land on my back gripping her tight against my chest. As soon as I hit the ground, my arms flew open, and she rolled away from me. And her dad turned to the terrifying site of his three-year-old, sobbing in the dirt.

The horse stood quietly, waiting to be told what to do next. I imagine she felt badly. She was one of the safest horses I had ever raised. It was not like her to lose a rider. She leaned down and nuzzled Lucy as she cried.

We were on an old logging road, lined with trees on either side, cut into a hillside two miles from home. Paul rushed to Lucy and began checking her over. Lucy was fine—unhurt—but I was not. When I tried to move, the world went black. There was something wrong with my back.

I told Paul to let the horses go. They would have to find their way home without us. He would have to go for help. After some discussion, Paul left Lucy with instructions to entertain me and started down the trail. Lucy, her crying forgotten, jumped up on a log and began turning pirouettes. Taking her assigned task seriously, she sang and danced for me as her father went for help. And then Paul was back, with Dave, far more quickly than he should have been. He'd met Dave just a hundred yards down the trail. Dave, wondering how our ride was going, had taken the golf cart out for a spin. He'd almost caught up with us by the time we fell.

Together the two of them tried to get me onto the golf cart but it soon became clear that I couldn't be moved. I blacked out any time we tried. Dave hurried home to call for help. We weren't sure what form that help would take. The last nine miles of our mountain road would take an ambulance an hour to make its way to us and the ride would be extremely bumpy. If I was seriously hurt, I wouldn't be able to manage the drive back down the hill.

Within fifteen minutes our neighbors, Bob, and Dynah, arrived. They were firefighters and worked as EMTs and first responders for anyone hurt on our remote mountain. They evaluated the situation, then went back down to our house (and the nearest cell signal) to make their report. We would need a helicopter. I'd injured my spinal cord for the second time in my life. I was going to need to be airlifted out of there.

In the meantime, more EMTs arrived. Eventually we had a good dozen people milling about, talking to me and each other. One of the young men went to his truck and took down a small teddy bear that was hanging on his rearview mirror. He gave it to Lucy and told her how brave she was. Lucy clutched the bear to her and basked in the attention of so many adults.

It took a while for the crew to figure out what to do. They all agreed I needed a helicopter, but we were in the woods on the side of a hill and there was nowhere for a helicopter to land. Eventually a plan was devised. They slowly and carefully rolled me onto a board. They duct taped my body, my head, and my face to the board so that I could not move my neck or back, and four of them lifted me carefully into the back of one of their pickup trucks. With a number of people working to keep me steady, the truck slowly crept further up the trail until it got to a place a quarter of a mile on, where the helicopter could land. I was loaded in and off we flew. The flight seemed to take only a matter of minutes. I could see nothing but the sky.

It turned out that I had a minor fracture of two of my vertebrae, the same two I had broken when falling off of Two-Bits ten years before. A broken back, but only a very slightly broken back. I didn't need to stay at the hospital overnight, but there was no way I would be able to traverse our road any time soon, so I went to my sister's house to stay for the weekend.

It was while I was laid up at my sister's house that Dave finally got a job offer after six months of being laid off. After I was healed enough, we made the slow, painful drive back to the ranch. We hired a neighbor to get us through until my back healed, and Dave flew to Chicago where he would live and work for the next four years. Six months Dave had been out of work, and we were behind on our mortgage with loans and credit card debt piled high. We slowly began the process of digging ourselves out of the mounds of debt left by Dave's time without a job. Money was so tight during those years that we had to be content with seeing each other only twice a year. We scraped together what we could to hire help while I healed. The horses needed to be fed and watered, fences kept in good repair and firewood brought in to heat the house. And I couldn't do any of those things. By the time I was walking normally again, my energy was so low I could barely leave the house.

143

Section Five

In A Hammock Chair On A Wooden Deck

45 years old - 50 years old...

I will not let what I cannot do interfere with what I can do.

(Edward Everett Hale)

144

CHAPTER 16

Overcoming Addiction

ourteen years Rajah gave to me, and never again did we see a hint of the aggression we had seen with Lamie. For those years, I did my best to love him as though he had never let me down. I couldn't imagine my life without him, but increasingly it became obvious that soon I would have to do just that. A night came when I knew the end was near. His muzzle had long ago turned gray, and his hind legs wobbled. He still followed at my side everywhere I went but now I watched carefully to see if he needed help standing or would be able to make the walk from the house to the barn. Fourteen years is old for a dog his size. We'd had him far longer than we could have hoped. It wasn't that he was sick. It was just that he was tired, so tired. And I knew his time was near.

One night, after Rajah had a particularly hard day of keeping up with me, I curled up next to him, stroking his gray muzzle and his velvet ears. It was clear he was in pain, and it was clear that he was ready to be done with this body, this life that wore on him so these days. My heart was breaking as I curled up against his old body on the floor beside my bed. "It's okay," I told him, "I know it's time for you to go. You have protected me all of your life and now your job is done. You are my precious companion, my perfect dog. I am safe now and I will be okay without you."

The next morning, trembling with the effort, he followed me faithfully to my truck. I struggled to lift him into the front seat. I had horses to transport that day and he loved driving anywhere with me. I would let him do this thing he loved one more time if he could. Sometimes he liked to sit up and hang his head out the window. But not today. Today Rajah sighed contentedly as he settled in beside me and rested his chin on my knee. As we drove, lying beside me in his favorite spot, Rajah, my perfect dog, slipped peacefully away.

* * *

Life was hard. We were drowning in debt. Dave was gone not just for a couple of weeks but for the foreseeable future. I was alone recovering from two fractured vertebrae and struggling to hold my health together. Rajah had just died. We had loans from banks, family members and friends. We had refinanced our mortgage to get back on track there but catching up had used all the equity we had in the ranch. Yet still, on particularly hard days, I would drive to town and buy flowers, books, or good food. I would buy clothes online or order something from Amazon. Sometimes I would overdraw our checking account and I had taken to lying to Dave about what I was spending. I had taken to lying to myself. But I couldn't stop. And I didn't know why. If I tried to deny myself my treat, I would become short of breath, panicked. I paced the house, unable to accept my life. I felt like I was literally going to die.

I got my first clue as to what was going on when I went to Overeaters Anonymous with a friend. She had been struggling with her weight and nothing seemed to work. She had started to think it might be an addiction. She wanted to go to a meeting but was nervous to go alone, so I went with her. They did a "first step meeting" in which everyone talked about the experiences which had brought them there. When we left, we sat in the car, silent for a minute. "It really seems to fit you," I said. "What do you think?"

She agreed. They had described exactly what was going on with her. It was an addiction she was fighting; she was sure now. And will power alone never won against an addiction. I started to drive her home. After a minute, I said, hesitantly, "You know, it sounds an awful lot like me too. Not with food, I mean. But with spending. If you applied it all to spending."

"Yes," she agreed, "I was thinking the same thing."

I was desperate to find some way to stop my behavior. So desperate that, despite being scared by it, this glimpse of an explanation gave me hope. I set about learning more about twelve step programs. Could I have an addiction? An addiction to buying things or getting a treat or…something. I found Debtors Anonymous and shortly after that I conjured up the courage to go to a meeting. I was nervous and defensive, as is everyone who walks through those doors. But I was also desperate.

There was a small meeting near my home which met in a local church. Four people sat around a folding table and welcomed me in. We recited the opening statements, and they began to talk about the program and how it had helped them, why they had needed it and more. At that time, I didn't yet own a smartphone and really wanted to buy one. But we were broke and couldn't afford it. As I sat in the meeting listening to people describe my same experiences in their lives one of the things they talked about was the program's prescription to track every penny you spend. I started to get excited. This was it, the reason I needed an iPhone. Sure, a pen and paper would do, but a smartphone would take my recovery to a whole new level, I was sure. Clearly, it was essential to adequate record keeping. Maybe I should leave the meeting right now and go right out and buy one?

As soon as I had that thought, the absurdity of it struck me. Here I was using a meeting of Debtors Anonymous to justify buying something I couldn't afford and would have to go further into debt to acquire. It became clear to me that I needed to attend these meetings regularly. I needed to commit to this program. I found it annoying—too based in religious language I didn't like, too kitschy and full of pat sayings. But I did it anyway. It was the only hope I had of getting my life under control.

It was the lifeline I needed. As part of the twelve steps, I set about trying to understand what had brought me to this place in my life. I came to realize where my addiction had come from. I had done this to myself. On purpose.

I saw myself back in my mother's house at 26, tucked in tight beneath a pink and gray quilt amidst soft pillows with a window overlooking the yard. I lay in bed for weeks, too tired to move. I lay there and I thought about the life I had just lost, my cabin, my ranch in Colorado. I mourned what I'd lost and tried to picture a future I could get excited about. But no pictures came. What if this was all I ever had, this illness, this exhaustion, this bed? I couldn't do it. I couldn't live with that. And so, I created an addiction.

I would get my treat every day and when I did, I would be happy. As long as I got my treat, everything would be okay.

At the time, I didn't know that it was an addiction I was creating. All I knew was that it worked. I had something to live for. And as time went by my need for a treat escalated.

On really bad days the need for the treat would overwhelm me and I would go out and buy hundreds of dollars' worth of stuff—a whole remodeled bathroom or new sheets for all the beds. Clothes. Make-up. Furniture. We started piling up thousands of dollars of credit card debt I could hardly explain. No matter how hard I tried, I couldn't stop. When Dave and I moved in together he had a strong savings account and investments in many places. It took only a few years for all that to be gone. I didn't know what was happening. I had incredible will power in most of my life. Why not with this? I just couldn't stop myself. Why was I so weak when it came to spending?

Finally, I remembered that day in my mother's house, under that pink and gray quilt, when I first created this addiction, complete with endorphin rushes and physiological changes that buoyed my mood and acted like a drug, giving me a high of my own making. Like the red dresses that hung in my closet, unworn and expensive, my treats had provided me with a way to hope, to live, to believe in life again. But they had wrecked havoc on the rest of our life. And it had to change. It was time.

I attended meetings. I worked the program. I hated it. At first, I was sure that nothing set up for other people could work for me without a great deal of adjustment. I was so different from other people, after all. There were my health problems. And my ADD. I would need to alter the Debtors Anonymous program to fit me, but, seeing no other options, I grudgingly decided to give it a try.

Altering the program didn't work. It took me a couple of years to realize that I was not as special as I thought. The program needed to be followed exactly as it was created. It was a common thing that I was doing; to assume I was too special to fit a pre-made plan. They called it Terminal Uniqueness. Many of us went through this phase and none of us found answers in the program until we let go of our imagined uniqueness and followed it exactly as written. And what do you know? When I followed it exactly as it was designed to be followed, my life began to change.

We were eight years into our time in Montana when Dave took a new job in Chicago. For four years Dave lived in Chicago, unable to come home more than twice a year. My health was rocky, with lots of ups and downs. But slowly, as I worked the program, I began to get a hold on my insane spending. Our financial life went from spiraling out of control to being stable and sane for the first time in years. At first, I was afraid. If I took away my addiction, I would take away my high. What if all that was left was that soul crushing depression that defeated my desire to live?

I took the leap anyway. I began to build a life without this addiction. I called my sponsor every day and followed the program's rules to the letter. And what do you know? I didn't fall into depression. I was elated. I was so relieved to be making my out-of-control finances sane again, that life looked *better* than it had in years.

CHAPTER 17

My Mothers Unwavering Spirit

M y mom came out to the ranch every summer. She was small with short, wavy hair and a ready smile. She claimed that she was never a mountain woman. She couldn't chop wood or haul water. But when we first moved out here, she was in the process of leaving active ministry. Mom had been a church pastor for forty years and now she wanted to focus her time on writing and leading workshops around the country. She wanted to spend time with her grandchildren and have a place to live a contemplative life. She wanted somewhere she could simplify her life, disconnect from society and technology, and focus on prayer and the present moment. Maybe not for the whole year, but for part of each year. She decided that living in an off-grid cabin on our ranch would do and began spending summers with us. Her wife, Sue, stayed in Iowa. She was younger than my mom and still worked, serving a local church as a pastor herself.

My mom's cabin had no electricity or running water, no indoor toilet, and was only marginally within shouting distance of the house. She cooked over an old Colman stove and watched out for bears and mountain lions. The cabin was heated with a wood stove, and she walked the quarter mile down the road to the house for showers and company.

I loved having my mom here. We had always been close and she was a pleasure to spend time with. She helped me when she could and supported me emotionally in all things.

Mom loved her little cabin. We had a deal that Dave and I and everyone else at the ranch would take care of her firewood and help her haul water, deal with any wild animal issues, and basically help her manage the rougher aspects of this life. And she would come to the ranch for three months every year and live here with her German Shepherd Dog. We would help her deal with mice and packrats. Mom joined us at the house for supper most nights, taking her turn on dishes and cooking just like everyone else. One night, just after dark, I was getting ready for bed when I saw her dog on my porch. She kept her dog with her at all times and I immediately worried that something was wrong. I pulled on a long coat over my flannel nightgown, stepped into my knee-high mud boots and lit a lantern. Then I called to her dog and tromped off across the field between the house and the cabin. Mom was waiting on the porch for me. She knew I'd come. She had let her dog out to go to do its business and for some reason the dog had headed back to the main house. "I knew as soon as you saw her you would be worried about me," she said as we sat on her porch and watched the stars. I stayed for a bit enjoying the night, then I re-lit the lantern and headed back across the field.

Another night I couldn't sleep so I spent two hours baking apple pies from scratch. When I was done, I decided I had to share them with somebody, wrapped one in a dish towel to keep in the warmth, and walked down the road to my mom's cabin. I didn't want to scare her by banging on her door so late at night, so I stood under her bedroom window and called until she woke up. Muddled and confused she came to the window. Upon seeing the pie, she immediately perked up. We sat at her kitchen table sharing the pie and watching the horses graze in the moonlight, then I headed back home and went to bed.

My mom has always been a talented minister with the ability to bring faith to life and make religion meaningful to all sorts of people. Her services are always powerful. There are sermons I heard her preach when I was a child which I still remember to this day. It wasn't long before a church in Missoula asked her to serve on their staff during the summers and for years, she has done this, preaching and leading workshops. She would go to town two or three days a week and stay at the ranch the rest of the time. She also wrote and published two books.

***

151

As I write this, my mom just finished her eighteenth summer at the ranch. For some reason, she seems to think she needs to go back to her house in the city during the winter months, but while the wildflowers bloom, she makes the ranch her home. She tells me I'm the Mountain Woman, not her, so I have to deal with mice and outhouse maintenance and any errant bears that wander through. But in truth, she is quite a Mountain Woman in her own right. She is seventy-six and lives with Parkinson's disease, and yet still she lives for months in a simple cabin which she heats with wood. For the past few years, she has said that she doesn't know if each year will be her last time staying at the cabin. It's not an easy life. But so far, she still comes out and walks the quarter mile each way to the house at least twice a day. So far, she keeps her fire going and cooks over her Coleman Stove and bars the door against bear every night.

***

We learned about the Parkinson's disease about five years into our Montana life. I was in my thirties. For a few years, my mom had developed a tremor in her hands which we thought was just an essential tremor, not connected to any other problems. She said her doctors had tested her for Parkinson's and ruled it out. But over the course of a couple of years, other things started to change. She worried about everything, even things she couldn't possibly affect. And not just worried but obsessed. Suddenly, my positive, brave leader of a mother didn't seem to be able to handle even the simplest of things. She was negative about everything, always focusing on what could go wrong. She was critical of strangers and everyone who wasn't family. She was only in her sixties, not yet old enough for us to be expecting many age-related changes. When she was at church all of this would fall away, and she became her competent, confident self again. But in her private life she was increasingly negative and afraid.

I felt like I had lost my mother. At this time, she had just begun spending summers with us at the ranch. I wondered if this was who she really was all along, and I was only just now seeing her as one adult to another. Could I possibly have been this wrong about who my mother was all these years? I was heartbroken.

Over time things got worse. She would become so focused on whatever was worrying her at the moment that she didn't see anything else that was going on around her. After three years of this I was at my wit's end. I didn't know what to do. And then one day while visiting my sister, my mom had a panic attack that lasted three days. She couldn't function. She couldn't be alone. My sister and I took turns sitting with her, singing hymns, and holding her hands. My sister finally recognized that something important was going on. She didn't ask. She told my mom that we were going to take her to the doctor.

At that point, my mom broke down and admitted that she had just gone to the doctor. And the doctor had insisted she get tested for Parkinson's disease. She refused but that visit had brought on the panic attack and her paralysis of the last three days. She was terrified of Parkinson's disease. She had known three people who had this illness and all three had been unable to speak, eat or function on their own. For years, her doctor had been considering this diagnosis and for years my mom had been denying it with everything she was worth.

My sister and I took my mom to a neurologist. The diagnosis was clear. It was Parkinson 's disease. They started her on medication immediately. The medication was extremely effective. Within a couple of weeks, her tremors were reduced to almost nothing and she was her old self again. Yes, she had more anxiety than she used to, but she was able to see what was going on and deal with it rationally. My mother was sick and had a serious illness. But she was my mother again.

***

As my mom learned to live with her illness, adjusting to the increased fatigue and learning her body's new needs, I found myself in an unexpected role.

I had lived with the realities of a serious illness for years. I was able to act as a guide in some ways. This was the first time in my life I was able to be the leader, the caretaker of another's journey. Always I had spent my life needing help from others, especially my mom. In some ways, I had never truly felt like an adult in my life. Being able to help her navigate her own feelings and those of the people around her fulfilled some part of me I hadn't known was empty.

And there was a lot to navigate.

Deep down most people believe they are healthy because they are somehow virtuous—they do the right things, or they are strong enough. Even when they spend their lives taking care of someone else who is sick, loving them and supporting them, still under their deepest self is the belief that they are too strong to have this happen to them. When a person gets seriously sick their whole identity is shaken. How could *they* have failed in this way? It happens to other people, but not to me...

Someone who is newly sick has to deal with both ends of this phenomenon. They are devastated to discover that they can get sick too. And they begin to see in other people, even their biggest supporters, this insidious belief that they, the healthy ones, couldn't ever get sick like that.

And then there's the practical stuff: We manage when we *can't* do something to ask for help. But it's not always that clear cut. There are the times when you could, technically, get it done yourself, but you know that you shouldn't because your body needs to rest. How do you ask for help then when everyone else is tired too?

And there are the normal things, things most of us expect with a change like this: anger for the changes, grief for what you've lost, fear for the future.

154

There are the practical challenges an illness brings to everyday life: becoming exhausted more easily; finding yourself unable to think clearly when exhaustion sets in; having to accept that during those times you may not be safe driving; needing naps during the day; never knowing, as you prepare to stand up in front of a congregation full of people, if your tremors or your fatigue will hit you so hard you can't function, or if you will get a second wind and sail through what you need to do.

On this sort of thing, I was an expert. And I found it meaningful that I had this to offer someone—that I who always needed, had this to give.

My mom is well practiced with Parkinson's by now. She knows what to expect, how to limit herself and when to ask for help. Her doctors say she is doing wonderfully, though the losses are still glaring to her. But the truth is, once she stopped denying it and faced what was happening, she returned to being herself—strength, grace, and courage in a little package. She writes honestly and bluntly about her struggles coming to terms with her illness and those writings helped others, as her life has always helped others, to find their spiritual center.

In the meantime, every summer she shows up at the ranch. She no longer drives herself the 1400 miles to get here. But she gets here, one way or another. And she tucks into her little log cabin with her outhouse and her wood stove and walks back and forth between the cabin and the house. She preaches on Sundays and leads workshops with titles like, *"I know We Are all Welcome at the Table but Do I Have To Sit Next to You?"* And she changes lives. She sits on her porch in the morning and watches the horses run, drinks tea with guests at her kitchen table and naps in her little twin bed under mounds of covers. In the evenings, she joins us at the big house for Beer:30, that time of the day when all the work is done and we gather to sit on the porch and drink lemonade, beer or whiskey, depending on our inclination. Mom drinks root beer and afterwards, helps make supper. On days that are too much, she cries, and on days when she has extra energy, she uses it to help me in whatever way she can—cleaning my room or straightening my office, helping me plant my garden or watering the flowers around the yard. For most of my life, when things have fallen apart, it is she who has been there to pick up the pieces and painstakingly glue them back together again. She still does that. But less. And at times we do it for each other.

***

A few years ago, we had someone living on the mountain who was volatile and unfriendly. He drove aggressively and resented the existence of other people, and he carried a shotgun everywhere he went. One morning we were out on a walk, myself and my friend, Karen, and my mother. My mom was a little wobbly that day and was walking with a walking stick. I was using a walking stick as well, just to help with my energy. We had five dogs, a cat, 2 geese, 2 donkeys and a turkey with us that morning. We made quite a procession going down the road and not a little roadblock. Suddenly, roaring towards us came the new neighbor in his pickup truck, tearing down the old country road at top speed. We stumbled to get out of the way, but wrangling all those animals is no quick job and he barely missed hitting the lot of us as he thundered through. In anger, I threw out my walking stick to slow him down, connecting solidly with the side of his truck. It slowed him down. He screeched to a halt.

The man was six feet tall and muscular. He jumped out of the truck in a rage, holding his shotgun in both hands. He came at me, screaming, with spittle flying every which way. His eyes were wild. I had dealt with men like this before and knew that they were dangerous. I also knew I would do best if I had only myself to worry about and I shouted at the others to go home. Karen took me at my word and disappeared down our driveway. My mom ignored me.

As the angry man charged me, I began to calculate what I needed to do in this situation to strike a balance between aggression and peace. (Too subservient and it would be like running from a dog. It would trigger him to become more aggressive. But at the same time, someone needed to deescalate

156

the situation.) I stepped up, preparing to do battle, and my mother, five foot two and wobbling on a walking stick, pushed her way in front of me. She threw up her arms like she was a basketball player blocking a shot and planted herself between the angry man and me. I was exasperated. What did she think she was doing? I moved her to the side, trying to place her behind me. Didn't she know it was harder for me to protect her and me both at the same time? She pushed herself in front of me again. Didn't she know I needed her to stay behind me in case he got violent? Didn't she know she was unsteady on her feet and wouldn't be any use in a fight? Our roles had changed. It was my job to protect her now. Didn't she know that? Hadn't she gotten the memo??

She hadn't gotten the memo. She didn't know. She knew only one thing—she was my mother. And no crazed man with a shotgun was going to get a clear shot at me while she was still breathing. Eventually the situation got so absurd that the man climbed into his truck and drove away. And I turned to my mother. *What the heck*?? What was she thinking? I drew in an exasperated breath, ready to berate her for her foolishness. Her eyes were wide. She still stood in front of me, hands outstretched to block anything bad from reaching me. And I saw it there. The mother inside. Nature's most powerful force: Wobbling on her feet, needing a walking stick, tiring easily and unsure what the future would bring, her body was slowing down. But that inner strength and passion that burned, that told her who she was, had not gone out. It burned stronger than her body could hold. And I saw it there as I opened my mouth to scold her for her foolishness. I saw it and I closed my mouth. After a moment, I stretched out my hand and helped my mother home.

CHAPTER 18

Twelve Years In

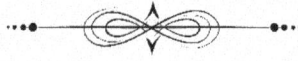

Twelve years we had lived in Montana. Our finances were difficult but, as I followed the Debtor's Anonymous program, we were no longer hemorrhaging money. We were slowly building up a financial base, slowly paying off our debts. We were stable once more.

Dave got a job offer for a job in Denver that would allow him to work from home. By this time, we had a full, almost normal electrical setup at the ranch. We used blenders and the occasional microwave. Life without electric lights was a distant memory. We had built Dave an at-home office in the loft upstairs and he was able to run his computers from there. We still didn't have very strong internet. There just weren't many options for a remote property like ours. We were able to find a plan that barely allowed him to work for $300 per month and we struggled through, with Dave going to town on days when we couldn't get enough bandwidth at home.

At this time, I was spending three days a week in Missoula, babysitting or just hanging out with my nieces, Lucy, and Ella. I had cut back on my business significantly because my energy just wasn't good enough to add that to the mix. I had gotten to the point where I was weary all the time, even on "good" days and I walked around with a heavy exhaustion sitting on my lungs pretty much constantly now. I no longer rode horses much unless I was taking someone else out and more and more, I felt a low-grade panic on those days, like I just wasn't up to the mental and physical energy it took to manage those rides safely. During the winters, I was now almost entirely housebound. I no longer had the energy to trudge through snow and wind to reach a fence that was down. In fact, I no longer had the energy to do much of anything during the winters. Just putting on my winter clothes, boots and snow pants and heavy winter coat would wear me out and by the time I got ready to go outside I was already too tired to do anything. So, most winters I did very little around the ranch. I even started to think about whether living at the ranch was really the right thing for me at this time in my life. Summers were still wonderful, but they were short and often too full of demands for me to properly enjoy them. I no longer had time to sit on the porch and watch the horses run. I was pretty unhappy during this time but was too busy trying to survive to notice it.

It was about then that we heard of a CFS/ME clinic at Stanford University that was getting national attention. I had never before worked with a doctor who knew more about my illness than I did. We contacted the clinic and were put on a waiting list. It took two years to get me into their program. In the meantime, my care came, as it always did, from my general practitioner. Mostly I was told to sleep (or not—some doctors insisted I shouldn't sleep as much as I did), eat good food and exercise.

Though I no longer did as much riding, I had fallen in love with horse packing—camping with horses. A couple times a summer, I would load my gear up on a pack horse, jump on Lady, my primary riding horse, and ride out for a night or three. I started off doing this from the ranch and soon got good enough at it to trailer to some of the extended wilderness areas which Montana claimed, sometimes spending a week out on my own with just my dog, my horse and me. Lady was a perfect companion for this kind of adventure, and she would stand guard at night, waking me with a snuffling huff if anything came too close to our campsite. I would hear her and crawl out of my sleeping bag, gun in hand, and shout in the direction she was looking, sending my dog out to chase whatever it was away.

I found these trips exhausting. And in some ways, they were miserable. I would ride a few hours in, then set up camp and sleep for the next few days until I was ready to ride out again. These trips pushed my abilities to the limit, but I craved the wilderness and craved every minute I spent out there alone, despite the physical misery. I would save all my energy to make a trip and then spend weeks recovering. But I lived for these trips and every chance I had; I went.

* * *

It's dusty in early August. The sun beats down. The grasses are dead or dying, crisp yellows and browns covering the landscape. The pine trees off in the distance are, as always, ever green. The land is dotted with cottonwood and aspen, beach trees and birch. There are large bushes, taller than a person, lining the banks of the river. Every few hundred feet, the bushes dissipate and there appears a rocky approach to the water. The water is a foot deep and thirty feet wide. The river winds and splits, making little islands here and there as it travels down the valley.

I am on one of these islands. We waded through the water to get to it. There are a few big pine trees, stout enough for a highline and my horses are tied by their lead ropes between two of these. My dog lays in the shade of another tree. My tent is set up just a short way away from the highline so that I can poke my head out in the night and check on the horses. I have a kitchen area set up on the other side of the island, far from where I will sleep, with a tall tree where I will hang my food bag from a sturdy branch.

The ground is sandy, in between the clumps of grass, and dust kicks up when the horses graze. During the heat of the day the air will seem so dry that I will need to sit in the river, water around my thighs with my knees sticking out to cool down. The intensity of the sun will be lessoned for a brief time by this but will return to torment me the minute I leave the river and go back to the land where I will be wet, and sand will stick to me. I am both elated and miserable: the heat, the bugs. I am uncomfortable as I sit, leaning against a rock or a log on the uneven ground. The sun bakes me and there is little shade to retreat to.

I love these trips. I wait all year for them. I crave them. But when they come, they are not always fun. Much of the time I am miserable. Or perhaps

I should say I am uncomfortable. I can't fully relax. I am either too hot or too cold. And my whole body aches with fatigue. It was exhausting to get here. It will be exhausting to get back. And rest here is not recharging. During the day, it is too hot to rest comfortably. At night, I am too on alert, listening for problems or danger coming my way.

In the evening, though, the air will cool slightly, and the sun will ease, and I will enjoy just sitting, leaning against a log, and watching the water drift by. I will let the horses off the highline to graze and follow them around the little island to make sure they don't decide to cross the river and leave me here. My dog will be done splashing in the water and come settle, quietly by my side, watching with me while the world turns. He has no ambiguity about these trips. They are heaven to him. And in ways, they are to me too. It is during these times that I remember why I came: the peace, the quiet. The stillness of it all. The rustle of the water. The horses grazing nearby and the dog by my side. It feeds my soul. If only my body didn't hurt so much. If only my muscles didn't cry out in pain and my lungs didn't ache. If only I wasn't worried about how I would do tomorrow when I head back, pack up my horse and ride for three hours. Will I be able to ride for three hours after so little sleep, with a body this worn down? I will have to. There is no other choice. The trail back is steep with a stiff climb on one side and a steep drop on the other. There is nowhere to stop and camp if I can't go three hours. I simply have to do it.

The nights are silent. Stars and Moonlight make shadows across the land. My horse snorts and I am out of my tent, looking in the direction she is facing, her ears alert and pointing towards something that concerns her. I am tense. I wait, listening to see if I hear anything. If I do, I shout and make some noise, then wait for my mare to relax again, telling me that it is safe to go back to sleep. But I rarely sleep well, waiting as I am for the next alarm. I've never seen any wildlife on these trips, never even seen a deer or an elk wandering. If the bear come by, they don't get close enough for me to see them, though I often assume that is what has alerted my mare and I carry a gun to shoot off if I need a noise bigger than my voice to convince a visitor to leave. But I get nervous at night. What if a bear did come? What if it is hunting and not just wandering through? That is rare and so unlikely. But in the black of night my brain plays what if games and I wonder.

In the morning, the air will be cool, and it will be hard to get out of my sleeping bag and start the day. But the horses will need to be fed and the promise of hot chocolate adds to the impetus to leave my warmth and get on with it. Besides, I need to pee. I pull on sweatpants and a fleece and if it's cold enough, a hat and gloves. Then I crawl out of my tent and greet the horses, who nicker in anticipation of their morning grain. I sit quietly by my camp stove after I have put out their food. The dog has eaten. I am waiting for my morning hot chocolate. I would enjoy these moments if I wasn't thinking so much about what comes next, about all the energy it will take to pack up and then to ride. I try to push my worries aside and breathe in the crisp morning smell of wilderness. I try to push away the future and enjoy the now.

***

I was looking for a Ritalin alternative to treat my ADD. Not all the time but when I needed to do a complex project that took focus and organization. Ritalin worked but left me shaky and we suspected it was doing damage to my adrenal system. My doctor suggested Vyvanse. I took it and overnight my fatigue went away. I was cured.

I lived the best summer of my life, riding horses, teaching students, going out with friends. I did everything I had ever dreamed of doing. And then it all came back. The Vyvanse stopped working and I was worse off than I had been before.

At first, I refused to admit it. I believed that I was still strong and full of energy. I couldn't accept that this wasn't the case. More than that, though, I truly didn't see that things had changed. I was so unable to accept that things were going back the way they were that I couldn't see what was happening right before my eyes. I pushed myself, refusing to see that I couldn't do all that I had done just a month before.

* * *

I was babysitting my nieces for a week while my sister and brother-in-law were out of town. I hit my limit of energy the day before they were due to return home. It had been one of the best weeks of my life—wonderful time spent with my nieces, reading bedtime stories, building blanket forts, and playing endless games of pet shop in which one of us was the pet shop owner, one of us was going to the shop to buy a pet and the third was the pet itself. The girls went to school during the day, and I slept until they got home, but even sleeping all day wasn't enough. By Friday of that week, I was fried.

Everything came to a head on Saturday afternoon when Ella, the youngest, refused to take a bath before bedtime. Her parents would be home the next day and the one thing I knew I hadn't managed well was keeping the girls clean. We had run through creek beds and climbed hiking trails. We were sweaty and probably stank. But Ella did what six-year-olds sometimes do—dug in her feet and refused to budge. She would NOT take a bath. I reasoned, I demanded, I cajoled. I yelled, I insisted. She didn't budge. Her sister tried to help but still, Ella wouldn't budge.

Finally, in desperation, I asked her, "What would it take to get you to take a bath?"

She thought about that. "You and Lucy take one with me," she declared.

Well, hell.

I hadn't taken a bath with the kids since they were babies. Six and eight years old. Isn't that a little old to be taking a bath with an adult?

Is it?

And just like that I didn't know. I had no idea if it was off the table or a perfectly reasonable request. I sat in their parents' bedroom, both girls looking at me expectantly and realized that I had no idea what to do and I had no idea how to find out what to do.

It isn't just that I wasn't sure. How can I explain it? I was completely blank inside. I had no idea how to go forward. I had no capacity to judge.

I have since read an article about CFS/ME research that talked about brain fog. Brain Fog happens when the executive functions of the brain (decision making, judgment) stop working. It all just goes away. But at the time I didn't understand that this vast nothingness had an explanation. I simply looked inside myself where my adult judgment takes place and found it empty.

* * *

We took our bath. Lucy and Ella and I, playing with bath toys and getting clean. Then the girls went to bed and the next day I went home. Shortly after, my sister called me. "Did you take a bath with the girls?" she asked. "Don't you know that is not okay?" I didn't. My sister's therapist wanted to call in social services, have this looked into. My sister talked her down. But this began what would eventually become a huge rift in my family, one which is to this day is not fully healed.

I was confused and worried. My sister was very clear that this issue was obvious. But no matter how hard I looked inside myself, it wasn't obvious to me. I couldn't find the judgment to tell me what I should have done. But why not? Why didn't I just know? Had I never been a competent adult? Had I somehow always been fooling myself and everybody else into thinking I was grown-up when really, I was just the immature kid I so often felt inside? I had assumed that everyone felt that way from time to time—like an imposter in the grown-up world. But maybe not. Maybe not having kids of my own had left me immature in some way that people who had their own kids no longer were. Maybe I really didn't know how to make good judgements.

It was years before I recognized what had happened that day. Years during which the same thing was happening again and again. Not with the girls anymore. I learned quickly on that one—when in doubt, go conservative. But that blank inside, that complete lack of ability to make a decision, was hitting me at other times as well. Mostly, it was hitting me while I was shopping.

I would shop all day until pretty soon I was too tired to function, but also too tired to know that I needed to stop. I would wander around a store in confusion, not knowing what I was doing there, putting things in my cart. Often it would get bad enough that I would not know who or where I was and I would stumble out of a store, my arms loaded with stuff I may or may not have paid for, knowing only that I had to get home. And I would drive home, often with no memory of that drive. I would come to our driveway, climbing out of a car, with no memory of how I had gotten there. This began to happen regularly but at the time, I didn't see it. I didn't notice. I didn't know it was happening.

CHAPTER 19

The River

Missoula, Montana is a beautiful town where three rivers meet. It is in a valley, surrounded by snow-capped mountains. During the summer months, every gas station and downtown shop rents inner tubes for floating the rivers. On hot summer days, people plunk down $15 and grab a tube, throw it in the river and float it downstream. Then they walk one of Missoula's many manicured hiking trails back to where they started, return the tube, and go about their day. A couple of times a summer, most people plan a full day on the river, and float for hours, winding the day away on peaceful, gentle water that is rarely deeper than their waist.

It was August. I was coming off of my Vyvanse months and still fighting to have my energy back. I was not aware yet how poorly I was doing. I was trying different dosages, desperate to get back the life I'd had in June. I didn't know how bad things were getting, or how bad they had already gotten. I denied that day by day I was doing more and more poorly, that the good time was done. I knew that nothing eased the constant pain in my body, the paralyzing exhaustion that made my muscles scream or the fogginess in my head. I was still pushing: Pushing to function, pushing to be independent, pushing, pushing, pushing. I was ignoring the pain and the exhaustion and trying to live the life I wanted despite the ever-increasing confusion that saturated my mind.

I'd floated the river every year since moving to Missoula, often with friends and family. I usually float the Clark Fork (the calmest of Missoula's rivers). I pick a day when temperatures are in the 90's and I zone out, cool and refreshed, floating quietly with the gentle current. There are always others on the river, lots of others, but somehow it still feels isolated and peaceful.

Somehow, I still get lost in my own world, even when my tube is tied to a friend's and we're floating side by side. In all the years I've been floating this river; I've never seen anyone wear a life vest. It would hardly seem necessary since 80% of the time you can simply stand up and walk out if you choose. Besides, the current is calm, and the water is peaceful.

Usually.

My sister insisted on lifejackets when I proposed taking her daughter on that year's float with me and some friends. At 12 years old, Ella had grown up on the river. They did more than tube floats. Her family owned a boat, and each member of the family had a carefully fitted lifejacket of their own. My sister talked to me about river safety and offered to send life jackets for the rest of our party. I thought this was a little ridiculous and felt a bit annoyed that she didn't trust me. I'd been doing this for ten years and there was nothing dangerous about the part of the river we floated.

Actually, I was more than just a little annoyed. I had been a lifeguard 20 years ago. I had the training to deal with an emergency. A little out of date, maybe, but that was the thing about me. I could always rise to the occasion when it really mattered. Yes, my body had been failing and I often struggled just to sit up. But when it really counted, I could always come through. In a true crisis, I could bring my people through anything, unscathed. On the river or off, her daughter was as safe with me as with anyone else in the world. And I was a little hurt that she didn't know that. Still, I gritted my teeth and agreed to take the lifejackets.

The day we went out was perfect. Temperatures in the 90's made the water heaven. The river was quiet and calm. We parked our pick-up car at the end of our route, then all piled into the drop-off car and drove to our starting point. My mom was coming with us, a rare treat since she was in her 70's and Parkinson's Disease limited her abilities at times. She was not very steady on her feet. But a river float didn't require her to be on her feet. We would tie her inner tube to mine and she could just sit back and enjoy the ride.

We got in the water and pushed off from the bank. Five minutes in, we realized that Ella and I had forgotten our life jackets. We left them in the car. Going back for them would have involved paddling to the side of the river and climbing along a steep bank all the way back to the car. I couldn't do it. What would my mom do while I went back for them? We compromised by letting Ella have my mom's life jacket (too big for her for sure but did that really matter?) and my mom and I went without.

* * *

We floated and talked and watched the bald eagles flying overhead. Once we stopped for a swim at a deep spot, letting Ella take off her life vest so she could dive and kick and play in the water like an otter. Besides, the vest really was too big for her and tended to push her head under water when she floated in it. She had mostly taken it off and just wrapped it around one arm, figuring it would do better to act as a floaty than a life jacket at that point.

As we floated, I remember thinking that this was one of the finest days of my life. The beauty of the mountains, the eagles flying, Ella and my mom beside me and the peace of being alone in my own head with the quiet and the calm. We floated for about five hours. We had barely a half an hour left to go.

As we neared the swimming hole that marked the end of our float, the current picked up and it began to be harder to control just where we went. Our tubes drifted towards the wooded banks of the river and my mom's tube began to push my mom nearer and nearer the bank. She began to get hit by tree branches and tangled in bushes. She called out for help, becoming increasingly agitated. That was my first clue—a clue that I missed—that I was no longer competent to be in charge. I watched my mom get caught by tree branches, saw her getting more and more upset by it, and I did nothing. I lay there watching, somehow unable to figure out how to act. My mind was simply blank. I had no idea what to do.

It shouldn't have mattered all that much—a few scratches from tree branches would have been all we had to worry about. Except that I was wrong about my sister's concern. She wasn't being over cautious. She wasn't expressing a lack of faith in me. She had taken river survival courses before buying her family a boat. She knew things about rivers I had never suspected.

Just as we reached the deep part of the river where we should have paddled to the side and climbed out, we hit a current we had not encountered before. It grabbed us and threw us onward. Within seconds, Ella's tube was ripped away from ours and she disappeared down the river in a rush of water. My mom began screaming her name. Then my mom's tube was ripped from mine and she began to disappear as well.

I watched, my mind numb, as my mom's tube was sucked into the current and whisked away from me. The ropes had released, and we were no longer tied together. I just sat there and watched, dumbfounded. My brain screamed at me that I had to do something, but it was like walking through molasses. I couldn't get myself to move. I couldn't get my mind to move. Then finally, with my mom's screaming and Ella gone, I gathered everything I had to take myself to that place of power where I always went in an emergency. I threw myself out of my tube, ready for the adrenalin to kick in. And I sank.

I had known for years that my energy was prone to crashing, that I couldn't count on being able to function after a long day. I had many times pushed too far and collapsed and been unable to move, unable to speak or get help for myself. I knew my energy was at a low point that summer and wouldn't last very long. But I also knew that in an emergency, I could set all that aside and do what had to be done.

I knew that. It was who I was. I was Good-In-An-Emergency. Always.

But this time there was no adrenaline. There was no burst of clarity. Barely able to think, my body not only didn't rise to the occasion—it didn't rise at all. The water in that spot was only up to my waist, but the current was so strong it pulled me over and no matter how much I fought, I couldn't stay on my feet. Ten feet away, young kids played in water that lapped gently around them, but right here, right now, I was going to drown.

I couldn't get my feet under me. With all my heart and all my soul, I wanted nothing more than to just let go. My brain screamed at me: *You have to help Ella! You have to help Mom!* But the vast majority of me didn't care. I had no hidden reserves to call upon. I was fighting with everything I had in me just to remember that I needed to try.

Dragging my will like a lead weight, I forced myself to act. I struggled to the surface and looked out over the water. Ella was too far away for me to see. My mom was still screaming, "Get Ella! Help Ella!" As I watched, my mom toppled off of her tube and plunged into the water. One hand grasped the air above the water, and she disappeared.

That was the last I saw of her before I was sucked down as well. And right then, with the image of her hand flailing above the water and the sight of Ella disappearing over the horizon, I realized that this time, I would not be able to rise. I was no help to either of them. If I didn't focus all of my attention on getting myself out of the river, I was going to drown. Even then, I wasn't sure I could do it, wasn't sure I could get myself to the shore. But I knew, *knew* that there was nothing I could do for my mom or Ella. My need didn't matter. My body simply didn't have it to give.

I considered letting go. If I was going to lose them, did I really want to live through that? But I didn't know for sure that I would lose them. What would it do to them to survive this and then lose me? I couldn't give up without knowing. I owed it to them to try to live.

I gathered up everything I had inside me and focused it on my own survival. In that moment, I turned my back on my mom and Ella. I simply put their fates out of my mind and focused everything I had on me. A voice in my head screamed and screamed. *This is not okay! This is not how it was supposed to be!* But I had no choice. I had nothing to give them. No matter how important the stakes, their fates were out of my hands. Period.

The current pulled my legs out from under me, and I plunged into the water again. I knew I couldn't fight it, this current. I let the current take me and focused on getting my head above water. Slowly, I worked my way sideways, towards the bank, all the time seeing in my mind, my mother and Ella disappearing in the distance. Then all at once, the current let me go.

I was still in water up to my hips, but the current was gone. Now it was just a matter of walking out of the river. Except that I was so weak, I couldn't walk. I turned, now that I could, in the direction the others had disappeared. Far down the river I saw Ella, calm and still holding onto her inner tube, making her way towards a stranger, a woman, who had swum out to help her. I saw my mother clinging to another stranger.

I sank to my knees. My legs wouldn't hold me. I knelt there for a while gasping, watching the two strangers slowly work their way to the shore with two of the most important people in my life.

I forced myself to stand. One foot. Then another. I watched my mother, clinging to the man who held her, slowly moving towards the shore. I watched my niece and the woman she held onto fight their way further down the river. I forced myself to keep going, one step at a time, though all I wanted to do was fall right there and let the water take me.

The man who reached my mom saved her life. She had gone under and had no ability to get herself above the water. Her legs wouldn't hold her. He reached her just as she went under for the second time, his strong hands reaching down to pull her up. "Don't drop me," she begged, clinging to him. "Don't let me go."

He didn't let her go. He fought his way back to the shore, holding her up, dragging her with him, until they were both on the bank and safe. His wife, meanwhile, had gone after Ella. Ella probably would have been fine if she had not had help, though she would have been swept far down the river before the current let her go. As it was, the woman who went to her held her in place until, together, they could get out of the current and make their way back to the bank.

These two people were there when we needed them most. They helped us to the shore and then went back to their kids, playing in the peaceful waves by the water's edge. And we never even learned their names.

I went home shaking and confused. The shaking went away after a few hours of sleep. The confusion lasted longer. It took a long time, more than six months, to really understand what happened that day. It took me that long to come to terms with it, be able to face it.

Now I know that that blank inside me is a warning sign. It means I have used up all my energy and crashed. It means I am no longer able to make simple judgments or decisions. At the time, I didn't know that. We hadn't discovered yet that I was having these spells where I became unable to function as an adult. We didn't know, and so I didn't see the warning for what it was. We didn't understand yet that my illness had progressed to a point where there was a cognitive component to the impairment I was experiencing.

I still have nightmares about the river. I still play that moment over in my mind when my mom and Ella needed me, and I couldn't be there for them; when there was nothing I could do. Though I haven't returned to the river since that day, I took a water safety course and learned more about river safety, just in case. I now own my own, carefully fit life jacket. And I am much more inclined to listen to my sister these days; less inclined to assume she is slighting me and ready to listen when I disagree with something she says. The truth is, I am the one who slighted her, not trusting her to know what she was talking about, assuming that her words came from her not knowing or respecting me. I owe her an apology for that. I haven't given it to her yet.

CHAPTER 20

The Mountain

I Crave the wilderness. I crave the untouched spaces where no roads cut the hillsides, and everything is wild for as far as you can see. The problem is getting to the wilderness. It was October and my energy no longer allowed much in the way of hiking. But riding—I could take my horse deep into the forest. She was my legs, the body which carries me to the places my heart desires. I couldn't ride for six hours like I had been doing during the summer months, but an hour or two I could manage and this I did whenever I could. It was one of the few balms to the constant anger I felt at the return of my illness.

I am lucky to live in a place with some of the largest wilderness areas in the United States. In the Bob Marshal Wilderness Complex, you can ride for days and never see an object made by people. If you're hardy. If you're careful. The Bob Marshal Wilderness Complex is not for anyone who isn't prepared to plan thoughtful, careful trips. It has one of the most active grizzly bear populations in the country, as well as black bears, mountain lions, wolves, and moose. To even get into the Bob Marshal, you have to scale high mountain trails with steep drop-offs, make your way carefully across scree fields and ford rivers. (Scree fields are rock debris that has fallen down mountain sides.) The deeper you go, the rougher the terrain.

I usually go into the Bob with friends, but this fall, a couple months after the river trip, no one was around to go with me. And besides, I had been wanting a chance to do a trip alone. I was still insisting that my energy was as good as it had been that summer when I took Vyvanse. Yes, my energy was slipping, but wasn't it just yesterday that I was riding fifteen miles a day and feeling better than I ever had? I'd had two months in the past summer when

173

I felt as though I had no illness at all. My energy was good day after day, until it wasn't. Still, I was sure if I just hung onto the good time with all my might, it wouldn't slip away.

I picked a new area of The Bob Marshal Wilderness I'd never been to before. I pulled into the horse-friendly campground and settled my horses into the corals available for public use. I chatted with another couple doing the same. They invited me to their trailer and showed me their map, pointed out a trail I might like to try. I looked over my options and made my choice. But I've never been very good with maps.

I knew that my energy was good enough that I could ride about five miles a day before I got too tired to manage on my own. Not the fifteen miles I'd been riding two months before, but still a respectable ride. I picked a trail I thought was about that long.

It was a perfect day when I set out the next morning. The other couple had already left. I saddled up my riding horse, loaded my pack horse, and hit the trail. We wandered quietly down a path with a forest of tall trees on one side and a steep hillside on the other. We crossed an old wooden bridge over a small stream. Our trail wound back and forth up the side of a mountain through quiet woods. There was a waterfall running off to our right. It was everything I wanted it to be.

Three hours later we had passed through deep forests, over steep mountain sides, and walked through the eerie blackened graveyard-like forests which had been hit by a forest fire the year before. Huge trees, still standing, all silent and dead, with thick blackened trunks rose amidst an otherwise empty landscape. I was loving the ride and the time in the wilderness, but my body was really starting to struggle. The ground was thick with compacted ash and dirt. This was not an area that was safe for stopping. Though it was the flattest area I had seen so far, the dead trees were prone to falling and not safe to camp around. I looked at my map, exhaustion beginning to muddle my brain, and saw that I had come only half the distance I had planned. I had read the map wrong. My intended camping spot was not five miles in but ten. I was never going to make it to the mountain lake which had been my destination. I would look for a safe place to camp before that.

That was easier said than done. I had ridden a total of eight miles before I came upon the first viable campsite on this trail. I had been climbing steadily over steep switchbacks all morning. On the uphill side, the mountain went almost straight up. On the downhill side, it was often a drop hundreds of feet to the river below. I had just passed between two mountains, walking through a little stream that crossed the trail and entering a scree field with a sheer drop off. I made my way through the scree field slowly, letting my horses find their footing carefully among all the loose rocks, and finally the sheer drop off to my right began to lessen. It became a narrow valley that led to the top of the mountain. There I found a pretty little meadow at the top of a rise, teeming with wildflowers and scattered with aspen trees. Exhausted, I pulled myself off of my horse. As often happened when I overdid it, my legs gave way and I found myself on the ground, underneath my horse. I lay there for a time until my strength returned. Lady stood patient. She was used to this.

When I could finally stand again, I pulled myself to my feet. I was discouraged and worried. My body felt like it weighed a thousand pounds. It felt like I was walking through molasses. Every step took effort. I struggled to set up my electric fence and settle the horses in to graze. Then, stumbling in my exhaustion, I got myself ready for the night. I put up my white and purple one-person tent and blew up my sleeping pad, almost crying with the effort it took to inflate it. I threw the sleeping pad down on the tent floor, grabbed my sleeping bag and climbed inside. I was too exhausted to eat.

I knew, as I lay there, that I was in trouble. I was that bone-aching tired that took days to recover from and left me fuzzy headed and weak; the kind of tired where my body hurt in every way, and it would be impossible to sleep. And because I wouldn't sleep, by morning I'd be worse. I pushed back panic, but deep inside I knew this wasn't good.

I had intended to spend three days out, to ride a little further every day. I knew from the first night that I wouldn't be doing that. I knew I was soon going to be too tired to take care of my horses or myself. I knew I had to get off that mountain the next day as soon as I was able.

As I had known would happen, I slept little that night. My body simply hurt too much to sleep. As morning dawned, I gathered myself to push through the exhaustion and the pain and get myself off of this mountain.

It took everything I had to pack my gear and get my horses ready to ride. I was tired and in a hurry. I had to keep going, pushing myself relentlessly, to get out of there before I found myself unable to move anymore. I didn't know if I would make it before I collapsed, so I threw everything into my saddle packs with no thought for the careful organization I normally used when packing. I didn't even double check my saddle to make sure it was tight enough. I just threw it on her back and climbed on.

The first stretch of trail left my little meadow and wound along the steep sheer cliff with a nasty drop into a river below. Normally, I loved places like that—places where even the established trails couldn't keep the wilderness from being wild. This time, as I rounded the first bend, I listed to the off-hill side and my saddle began to slip.

At first, I held on for dear life, trying to use the horse to keep myself from pitching over the edge. Then the horse started to come with me. Realizing I was pulling her over, I pushed myself out of the saddle and hit the ground. I rolled off the narrow trail and began to slide down the hillside, only stopping when I wedged my ankle painfully against a fallen tree.

I lay there, clinging to the hillside, breathing heavily. My horse stood above me on the trail, my saddle hanging under her belly. I dug my fingers into the side of the hill and took stock. My ankle had twisted, and I couldn't put any weight on it, but I was otherwise okay. On hands and knees, I started climbing my way back up the hill.

I reached the trail and sat for a moment, catching my breath. I was panicked and confused. My legs dangled over the edge towards the river below. My hands were scraped and dirty. My ankle throbbed. Finally, I hoisted myself onto my knees, then used the horse to pull myself to my feet. I clung to my horse's neck. There was no standing on that ankle, but I hobbled myself around to her side, holding to her as I tried to pull the saddle into place. I was crying, exhausted beyond measure and aware that I would not be able to get back on my horse with my low energy and my hurt ankle. I just wouldn't be able to pull myself up again.

Once I lost my balance and pitched over the side again, but I clawed my way back up and started over. I'd let the pack horse go, dropping her rope in the hopes that she would stay around her buddy and not wander off. And then, at the end of my own rope, so to speak, I tipped over the side again. I flailed, trying to grab onto my horse to keep from falling, but I was too far gone. I screamed as I tumbled down the hill.

Once again, I struggled my way up the hillside, using small trees and downed logs to pull myself up, digging in with my good foot to brace myself against falling back down. Finally, for the third time, I pulled myself onto the trail. For a time, I just sat and cried. I was exhausted and wanted to give up. Everything hurt and I wished I could curl up in a ball and sleep. There was no way I could walk beside the horses on this trail—the path was too narrow for two of us to move side by side. I knew that if I could convince them to leave me, my horses would follow the trail back to the trail head and wait for me at the trailer. In my confusion, this seemed like the right thing to do. So, I did what ended up being the stupidest move of the whole adventure. I smacked Lady on the rump and yelled until she reluctantly started off down the trail. The pack horse followed close behind.

So, I sat on the trail, dirt smeared down the tear tracks on my face, unable to put any weight on my ankle as I watched them go. And slowly it dawned on me what I had done. I didn't have my horses, just me and my dog, Kaladin, who had run frantically up and down the trail every time I fell. He sat now, up against me, looking into my face for some clue on what to do. Finally, I wiped the tears off my face and took a breath. It was time to take stock.

And that's when I knew I was really in trouble. I had not been thinking clearly that morning when I packed my horse in a hurry. I'd thrown all my gear on the pack horse. That included every piece of emergency gear I had with me. My first aid kit, my GPS emergency locator beacon which allowed my cell phone to work in remote areas, my warm clothes and all my food and water. All of this was on the horse which had disappeared down the trail and was gone. I knew better than this. I lectured other people about it all the time. You never put your emergency gear on the horse. The times you truly need your emergency gear, the horse is rarely still with you. I always carried my emergency gear in a backpack on my back. I was wearing that pack right now, but it was empty. That morning, I had been too tired to pull myself up onto my horse's back and had taken all the weight out of my backpack to make it easier to manage. I had my cell phone in my pocket. It had no reception. Everything else was on the horse.

I was eight miles into the wilderness with no expectation that anyone else would come along. I had no way to call for help. I was dressed in shorts and a tee-shirt. The nights regularly got down to the 20's. I couldn't walk on my right ankle. My mind was numb with exhaustion.

I took out my phone and tried three different people on three different texting platforms. I told them what had happened and asked them to call Dave. "Tell him that I'm not seriously hurt but I won't be able to get myself out of here and I don't have any of my emergency gear." None of the messages went through.

Eventually I stopped crying and stared out at the wilderness I loved so much. I didn't see the jagged peaks or wildflowers or the river down below. I saw only my own exhaustion and felt my own worry. I didn't know what to do. Should I try to make my way down the trail as far as I could go, knowing that Dave would eventually send someone looking for me when he didn't get my regular text. Dave and I had a deal that if I didn't contact him every 24 hours, he would call in a rescue team. By the next morning, I could assume he would act. But what about the night?

I could expect it to get down into the twenties in these hills at night. I could find food and water if I had to. I knew all about edible plants and how to dig for water. I had a lot of survival training. I could dig a shelter with my bare hands, maybe into a crevice between the ground and a fallen tree. But what I didn't know was how cold it had to get before my life was truly in danger. And though I knew how to find shelter I didn't know how warm such shelter might keep me and if it would be warm enough. What if, despite all of my supposed skills, I froze to death in the night because it was simply too cold for my body to survive? I imagined Dave, my parents and my nieces getting the news that I had frozen to death on this mountain side, and I knew that I had to keep trying to make my way out. I couldn't risk staying put.

Still in a sitting position, I began scooting down the trail, one step at a time, pulling my butt along with my one good foot. I walked like a crab with only three legs, lurching a few inches at a time. It was slow going but since it was only about ten am, I had the whole day to work my way towards home. When I made it to the creek that crossed the trail, I sat for a time to catch my breath, letting my injured ankle sit in the ice-cold water for a time. Then I dragged myself through the water and scooted on.

I made slow progress that way, scooting slowly along for ten or twenty feet, then laying back with my hair in the dirt to catch my breath and doing it all again. I was hours into my trek, and I hadn't gone even a fourth of the way. I was coming to realize that getting out this way, if I could even do it, might take most of the night, and my body already wanted nothing more than to lay down and give up. But I had to keep going one inch at a time.

It was early evening when I heard the beep, the sound of a text message going out on my phone. I grabbed for the phone. I had cell reception for the first time that day. The messages I had typed out that morning had gone through. Minutes later replies started coming in. Dave texted me back. "Do you need me to call search and rescue?"

Again, I thought about the option of staying the night here. I was not lost; I knew exactly where I was. I was on a well-maintained trail and had only to follow it to reach my truck. I was sure my horses would have followed the trail right back to the corrals they had stayed in the night before and it was likely that someone at the campground, finding them standing about riderless, would saddle up and come looking for me. But evening was coming on and it would be dark soon. I was injured in grizzly bear country. I didn't have my bear spray or my gun. I did have my dog. Kaladin had stayed by my side through all of this, never leaving me. He wore his own backpack. But it was empty. The food and water that should have been in Kaladin's pack, like the emergency gear that should have been in my own, were on the horse. And the horse was gone.

"Yes," I said, "I think I need search and rescue."

***

I told Dave exactly where I was and that I would continue to make my way towards the trailhead. As night fell, I became more and more exhausted and soon found I could barely continue my slow trek down the mountain. I would lay on the ground, gasping for breath for ten minutes or twenty, then slowly scoot myself another foot or two before I had to lay back again. It was dark when I finally heard the horses.

A man came around the bend leading three horses. I learned later that he was a park ranger in his seventies who had spent his whole career in these mountains. I couldn't see much in the dark and he used no flashlight. But I got the impression of a solid, strong man in jeans and a flannel shirt. He walked in front of three horses. ATVs couldn't make it to where I was, and the local search and rescue group had no one working this week who had horses available. He had heard the call go out for a rider on horseback to do a rescue mission and drove to the campsite where I had left my truck. The search and rescue people were already there. They had found my horses, untacked them, fed them and tucked them into a coral for the night. They gave the ranger the report and off he went to find me.

I was four miles from the trailhead when he got to me. I had crawled and dragged myself approximately four miles from where I had first fallen. The ranger helped me onto one of his horses and asked me if I thought I could hold onto all right to ride four miles out. I thought I could hold on as long as I needed to, I was so relieved to be on a horse again, and found, and in the care of someone who knew these hills so well. He used no flashlights but seemed to have no trouble navigating the steep trails in the dark.

He walked and I rode and slowly we made our way down the hill. Through the burnt-out forests and down the steep switchbacks, we walked confidently in the dark. Three miles later we met up with the search and rescue people who had brought their ATVs as far down the trail as they could go. They transferred me from the horse to an ATV, I thanked the ranger one more time and he left us, turning up a side trail and riding away into the night. It didn't faze him a bit that it was ten o'clock at night and pitch black out. He had a hunting camp to check on and, as he was already tacked up and, on the trail, he thought he would do the ten-mile trek tonight and check on the camp in the morning.

As the ranger disappeared into the darkness, I saw that there must have been a dozen search and rescue people on maybe four ATVs. They were all excited. One of them told me they had been called out three times this season, but this was the first time a rescue had actually been needed. They were all volunteers, and they were riding an adrenaline high. I had been dreading them, expecting them to lecture me about the stupidity of my decisions that day, about going into the wilderness alone and all the trouble I had caused. I was also dreading the bill. I had no idea how much rescues cost, but we didn't have the money to pay for one of that, I was sure. But every single person I talked to was kind to me that night, encouraging and positive with never a hint of disapproval or anger from any of them. And then their leader made a joke about the bill, and I must have looked pale because he said, "You know this is all free, don't you? We don't charge for rescues." Tears of relief and gratitude filled my eyes. I blinked them away.

I made it back to camp bathed in the goodwill and care of these people whose names I would not remember. My horses were content and well cared for. My gear was carefully stored in the tack room of my trailer. I called Dave and told him everything. We decided I would stay the night in my camper and drive home in the morning.

I dug out my sleeping bag, fed Kaladin and climbed onto the bed I kept in the back of my trailer. I fell asleep almost before my head hit the pillow. The next morning, I woke up grateful for the gift of life. I loaded up my horses and went home, where I fell exhausted into bed.

CHAPTER 21

My Greatest Supporter

I'd had a close call on the river and another on the mountain. My energy was low, too low to allow me to drive safely, but that didn't stop me. Instead of getting my attention, I had swept my misadventures under the rug, refusing to look at them clearly, refusing to see. I refused to slow down. I was angry. Never in my life had I been this angry. I refused to give in to this illness. I had seen what my life could be like without it and I could not accept these limits anymore.

And I was arrested for shoplifting. And finally, I saw. I saw that I was throwing a tantrum I had no right to throw: So, life wasn't fair. Who had said it ought to be? What right did I have to risk other people's lives just because I was angry at my own? The county prosecutor dropped the charges against me, and I went home and cried in Dave's arms. And I changed the way I was living my life. I quit the fight.

By then I hardly had a choice. I chose to stop fighting, but I wouldn't have had the ability to fight much longer even if I hadn't made the choice. My body crashed. It crashed hard.

I became too weak to sit up without help. I couldn't join my family for dinner around the table. I couldn't sit that long. And I couldn't stand. When we left the ranch, which was rare, I needed a wheelchair. I didn't have the energy to hold myself up without it. I couldn't walk down to the barn to see my horses. I couldn't handle the stallions. I couldn't teach classes. I lay in bed most of every day, too weak to read, too tired to watch TV. It was everything Dave could do to hold our lives together.

* * *

Dave eventually forgave me for the betrayal of the Walmart night. He got over his anger and took up his position at my back, guarding me, supporting me in everything both emotionally and physically. He again took over the shopping, the laundry and cleaning the house. He did all the cooking and washed all the dishes. He helped me move between the bedroom and the couch, brought me glasses of water with lemon in them and made me sandwiches, cut diagonally just the way I liked them. He also fed the animals and kept up on the work around the ranch. He had already been exhausted. Now it was worse. We knew this couldn't last.

Dave was bowing under the weight of all that was asked of him. I finally had to accept that the horse business, and most of the animals, had to go.

We sold the fourteen goats. We ate my beautiful, ugly turkeys. We found homes for the donkeys and the geese and gave away most of the chickens. We closed the business and sold the horses. I kept only Lady, my primary riding horse. She had let me know many years before that she was my horse and no one else's. She could read me like a service dog; knew when I was pushing too hard and when I was going to crash. She let me know by refusing to let me mount her when my energy was too low to be riding safely. It was the only time she ever refused me anything. She took care of me, would do anything for me, but threw a fit when someone else tried to ride her. The only times she would let other people ride her were the few times when, out on a ride with a friend, something went wrong with the friend's horse, and I decided we needed to switch horses so I could deal with a dangerous or difficult situation. But now I couldn't ride Lady anymore. I couldn't even go down to the barn to see her. But I couldn't give her up either. She was mine and I was hers. No matter what. Forever.

We simplified our life as much as was possible, given the off-grid horse ranch and the harsh Montana winters. I mourned the loss of my animals. We hunkered down and focused on surviving. Then we heard from the doctor at Stanford Medical Center outside of San Francisco who specialized in

CFS/ME. I had been accepted into his program. We went to San Francisco to meet with him.

Travel was barely possible for me at that point but with the help of wheelchairs and a lot of work from Dave, we got me there and back. The doctor said I had one of the most severe cases he had ever seen and spoke bluntly to me. A lot of his patients did recover but it was going to be a long shot for me. The only chance I had of ever getting any of my life back lay in accepting, for real and for always, that I had to slow my life down. I had to rest when I was tired, never mind if I was always tired for years on end. I had to stop pushing myself no matter what. Even getting up off the couch to get my own cup of water was too much right now, he told me. "You are tired, you ask Dave. You don't do it yourself."

He got through to me: he and the Walmart night. I was never the same after that. I had come to a profound acceptance of my illness. It was not an acceptance which came from peace and contentment. It was an acceptance which came from shame and relief. Several times I had survived what could have been disasters, with little cost to pay. I will never forget.

***

This change was reinforced by my suddenly having a doctor who encouraged me to listen to my body, not to just push through the hard parts and force myself to function. Most of my life, my doctors had instructed me to push myself to act normally no matter how I felt. "Just push yourself and you will be fine," they would say, or "You are clearly sleeping too much. Make yourself get up even if you don't want to." My new doctor railed against this advice, telling me that it was this kind of irresponsible action which would prevent me from recovering from this illness. "You're tired, you rest," he insisted, "Always. Every time. For as long as it takes."

He put me on a medication he believed would help. It was expensive—$12,000 out of pocket every three months, even with insurance. But it was the only hope I had of getting out of bed and being able to live my life again.

For five years, we took out loans and used credit cards to pay for groceries, freeing up every penny we could for my medicine. For five years, we had sunk ever deeper into debt. But slowly, I began to heal.

***

Life is hard. Our primary generator went out two weeks ago, and our backup generator went out the next week, along with the septic pump. We scraped together $5000 to replace the primary generator only to find that a replacement cost more along the lines of $15,000. We lost two horses this year including a baby I was raising for myself. She broke her leg, and the break was not one that would ever heal. Jana, my old German Shepherd who loves like no other being I have ever known, developed Vestibular disease and has trouble walking in a straight line. She still pours out joy like a puppy if anyone throws a stick or a ball near her, but her age is showing, and we know she won't be with us long.

Life is hard.

Spring was starting to show its face, even at the ranch, which sits at a high elevation where winter holds on long and hard. Snow and ice were finally melting, and the horses were beginning to shed their winter coats. As Dave and I drove home from town I watched eagerly out the window to see if any of the early wildflowers had appeared yet. "Oh look!" I cried at the bright yellow bells I finally caught sight of. "It's…" my mind blanked on the words, as it had been doing increasingly these days.

"Glacier Lilies." Dave supplied.

I looked at him in surprise, a smile creeping across my face. "How did you know that?" I asked, "You don't care about wildflowers."

He glanced at me before turning back to the road. "No," he said, "But I care about you. And you wait for them every year and you're always happy when you finally see them. So of course, I know their names." And just like that life doesn't seem so hard anymore.

CHAPTER 22

The Four Exceptional Dogs

You know that amazing, once-in-a-lifetime dog we all dream of? The one who lives for you, shares everything with you and possesses a soul as deep and rich as any human has ever had? Well, I've had four of them.

My first German shepherd was Rajah. He had a serious mind and thought deeply about things. He'd jump six feet into the air to catch a Frisbee. Night after night, on long backpacking trips, he'd sit sentinel outside my tent. He never let a horse and rider leave our barn without him.

My second soulmate was a 110 pound Rottweiler named Thor. I got him when Rajah was getting old, too old to protect me as he always had. Thor was all the protection I needed and gave Rajah a chance to relax in his last years without stressing about my safety, so long his responsibly.

Thor never had a deep thought in his life. He shook the whole house when he ran, and he did everything with all his heart. He lived for me every moment of every day, and he played like a rambunctious child. His favorite toy was a full-sized car tire, which he would wear around his neck for hours, then pull it off, grab it in his teeth and throw it over his shoulder so he could chase it down and pick it up again.

The third dog was not supposed to be one of those heart-tied bonds. I've had other dogs, dogs I loved greatly for years, who weren't quite what Thor and Rajah were. I expected Jana to be one of them—a normal dog for our family to love. But she was much, much more. I adopted Jana, a German Shepherd, when she was 6 years old. When she was two, she took 9th place in the world at the international Schutzhund competitions in Germany. She was extensively trained in personal protection, tracking and obedience. She

188

had spent most of her life as a high-quality breeding dog who was known for producing exceptionally good service dogs with the sensitivity for seizure alert. Under normal conditions, I could never have afforded a dog of her caliber, but the breeder who owned her wanted her to be able to retire and spend the rest of her life being "just a dog." She heard about my ranch, learned about my life, and offered me Jana at a price I could afford. The plan was that I would breed Jana once, keep one pup and sell the rest, then spay her and let her be just-a-dog for the rest of her life. All of this happened just as planned, except that the bond I formed with Jana was far more than I expected.

When Jana was nine years old, still carrying a ball everywhere she went and following me from room to room all day long, I was ready to take on my fourth once-in-a-lifetime dog. His name was Kaladin and he'd been in training to be a service dog since the day he was born.

Kaladin was Jana's son from her last litter. We chose him and made plans to enter a program which would guide me through training him. Unfortunately, right about that time was when I hit my big crash, a major setback with my illness which would last not days or weeks, but years. If I ever wanted to recover enough to live my life without a wheelchair, or be able to ride my horses again, I would have to spend as much time as was needed, a year or more, doing nothing more strenuous than sitting on my couch. Here was Kaladin, ready to go, and there was no way I could raise a puppy, much less train one as extensively as Kal would need to be trained.

Help arrived when we needed it most. We found someone who was willing to foster Kaladin and continue his socialization as he grew. We found a trainer we could hire to do all the training herself. We raised money to pay for Kal's training. It took two years, and, in the end, he was everything I'd hoped for. He'd been trained to pull a wheelchair, pick up things I dropped and go for help when I got into trouble. But the most valuable skill he offered me had to do with his seizure alert abilities. One of the hardest aspects of my illness is the "crashes," I experience in which I suddenly became unable to

189

stand or think clearly or, in recent years, even recognize who and where I am. These crashes happen without warning, and I can't predict them. They come out of the blue and leave me incapacitated and confused. Kal can alert me before a crash is coming on, allowing me to get myself into a safe situation. This effectively gives me back my freedom to go places independently.

Kal is a hit everywhere we go. He wears a leather and metal harness with a handle I can hold onto to steady myself when walking or provide support when standing up. His harness has a red, cloth vest on it with patches which say things like, "Service Dog" and "Do Not Pet." There are a lot of Do Not Pet signs, unfortunately. It's not that he wouldn't love to be petted, or that I want to keep him all to myself. It's just that when people pay attention to him it distracts him from his job. He gets excited and wants to greet everyone like an old friend. He focuses on them and not on me and he risks missing the subtle signals my body sends out which warn him that I am in danger. I used to let him greet people anyway, since it gives him such joy, but eventually I decided that it wasn't fair to him to allow such things. Blurring the lines between Work Time and Fun Time makes it hard for him to focus on his job. If he is constantly looking around, anticipating meeting his next best friend, he can't focus. But he knows he needs to focus, and ultimately it just stresses him out. So, I have taken to following Service Dog Etiquette to the letter and trying to make it more clear to him when he is working and when he is not.

Kal works when I go out, leave the house. At home, he gets to just be a dog. When I travel, he comes with me wherever I go.

On planes, Kal squeezes all 90 pounds of himself between my knees and the seat in front of me. He is so unobtrusive that the people around us rarely even know there is a dog aboard. Once when Dave and I were traveling together and there was a third person in our row, I leaned over to ask our seat mate if she was allergic or uncomfortable with dogs. I always do this, as I once sat next to a woman who was terrified to her very bone of Kaladin, and I never want to do that to anyone again. There is always someone who is willing to switch seats with a non-dog-lover. So, I asked our seatmate if she

190

was comfortable with dogs. The woman looked at me confused. "Why?" she asked. I motioned to Kaladin whom she hadn't noticed, and she gave a little shriek. "Oh, my goodness!" she cried, "I didn't see him there!"

We are constantly told how beautiful he is and everybody we meet wants to talk about him. When he's not working, he is just a big goof, obsessed with chasing balls and playing Stick. When he is working, he is serious, watching me, alert to everything. If he senses (smells? I don't know how he does it) a crash coming on he moves in close to me and looks me in the eye until I notice him. If I don't pick up on his signal right away, he lifts one paw and delicately sets it on my leg. He knows his job is to take care of me and gets stressed if I go anywhere without him. Which I don't for the most part. His ability to warn me before a crash is coming on is so valuable I keep him by my side. He slips between the pews at church or under the table at my favorite restaurants, watching me closely all the time. Unless there are kids nearby. Then he splits his time between watching me and staring longingly at them, wishing he could meet them, wishing he could play. A crying child is almost enough to make him break his training—almost, but not quite. He wines quietly as he stares intently at the child who clearly needs his help and he shifts uncomfortably, longing to go to them and lick their tears away.

He knows he is a protector, a caretaker, that this is his job. He knows I am his primary responsibility. But if my nieces are around, he will allow me to hand him off for a night or two to go on hikes, sleep in their beds and generally take care of them for a time. He adores them (and sleeping with them is the only time he is allowed on the furniture.)

And the rest of the time, when we are at the ranch and I don't need him in-vest and working by my side, he still takes it upon himself to make sure and tell me when I have spent too much time sitting still and need to get out in the yard and play. Kal has high hopes that if he keeps working with me, I will someday truly appreciate the true value of a good stick.

CHAPTER 23

Back In Business Again

$\cdots\bullet\hspace{-0.5em}\text{---}\hspace{-0.5em}\infty\hspace{-0.5em}\text{---}\hspace{-0.5em}\bullet\cdots$

After five years of resting, I was able to go off the medication that had pushed us so far into debt. By then our finances were ruined more than they ever had been before, with hundreds of thousands of dollars of debt weighing us down. But slowly, slowly, I was improving. First, I could sit up on the couch for most of the day. Six months later, I could stand long enough to make a cup of tea. Over the course of a few years, I slowly gained back some of my abilities. I could sit up at the table through a whole dinner. I could walk down to the barn again. I could go to a store without needing a wheelchair. One day I climbed on Lady's back, and we wandered around the yard together, my body laying flat against her, my cheek pressing against her neck, my legs dangling down her sides. I breathed that horsey smell and couldn't stop smiling. I needed help down off her back and was almost too shaky to make it back to the house. But it was worth it. Someday I would ride my horse again. I knew it. If only I could keep from taking on too much too soon, I would continue to recover.

And that was the doctor's constant mantra. *You will only get better if you can keep from doing too much. You don't push. You rest if you are tired, no matter what. And you don't exercise.*

Don't exercise. Have you ever heard a doctor say that? It turned out that CFS/ME has an unfortunate side effect. Exercise is harmful. Anything that gets my heart rate up causes me to crash, requiring hours or days or even weeks to recover. The doctor insisted that I leave all exercise for the time when I was recovered enough to handle it, and bluntly told us that this would take years.

I gained weight. For years, I lay around the house too weak to do anything but sit. Partly it was the lack of physical activity, but partly it was boredom too. The only thing I had to look forward to in a day was eating. I love gourmet food. A good, gourmet meal would make me happy for days and happiness was hard to come by with the state my life was in. Unfortunately, I didn't have the energy to cook gourmet meals most days. So, I fell back on treats; peanut M&Ms or mini vanilla cupcakes or Oreo ice cream. Anything to break up the excruciating monotony of my day. I, who had always been thin, was now fifty pounds overweight. Then more. I knew I had to get a handle on this, but I didn't know how. My doctor still insisted that I was not to exercise. When I asked him about my weight, he just said, "Don't eat so many treats."

Even when I ignored the no exercise rule, I could not walk more than a quarter mile. I could do more in water. For some reason water gave me energy without costing me so much. But the pool was an hour drive away and even if I had the energy to get myself there, I wouldn't have the energy to get back. Once or twice a season Dave would drive me to a mountain lake a few hours from Missoula, but those trips were few and far between.

So, my recovery continued but at a creeping pace, and always with my weight a constant battle I couldn't figure out how to fight. Progress was slow. Sometimes it felt like I was not making any progress, but then I would look back at how I was six months ago, or six months before that, and I could see that I was improving.

* * *

Finally, I got well enough to ride again and work with my horses. And then I got even better. I was strong, I had energy. Nothing like during the Vyvanse time, but I was able to function for much of each day. I had thought that I would never be able to run my business again but here I was, thriving. I was well enough to ride and to work. Lady was getting older, and I knew I'd need a younger horse soon. So, I bought a stallion to be my riding horse and to open up my business again. Just one stallion. Just breeding to outside mares. I'd make some money to offset horse expenses and help get us out of debt.

My cousin, who lived on the ranch with us, bought some goats. We got a few chickens.

During the darkest times of my illness, I had given up on ever being able to fill the ranch with animals again. Now here I was, stronger than I had been in years. Strong enough to ride a stallion and breed mares. For about three months. And then I slipped backwards again.

For no apparent reason, my energy just ebbed. I could ride Lady now, for half an hour at a time or slightly more. I needed help afterwards getting her brushed out and put up. I could only do that in weeks when I had nothing else to take my energy and could spend some days recovering afterwards. I chaffed to be able to go out for longer periods, but was also grateful to have this much, grateful that I hadn't slipped any further than I did. But then I spent the winter on the couch, unable to go outside for even the small amount of exercise I was allowed to get, and I slipped backwards more. I couldn't ride. I couldn't do anything but sit.

Always in my life there has been this back-and-forth struggle between getting better and getting worse. During the summers, I would do better, begin to build up my strength and improve, but then winter would come, and I would sit on the couch for six months and I would get worse again. When I had first moved to the ranch I was as active in winter as in summer. But now-a-days it took too much energy to pull on all of my winter gear. I would be exhausted before I even stepped outside. One winter I went to Arizona for two months. That year I continued to get healthier and didn't slide backwards as I usually did. But the next year we couldn't afford for me to travel.

As I write this, I have come to realize that in all my years of ups and downs I have never really understood the up and down nature of my illness.

194

I am ashamed, seeing this pattern so clearly laid out before me in my writing, that I didn't see it as it was happening. I always believed that how I am today is how I would always be. So, when I began to do well, I assumed I would always be that well from here on out. This despite the dozens of times I had done well in the past only to enter into the downward ebb of this illness and loose my abilities once more. If I were sick today, I believed I would always be sick. If I were strong today, I believed this was a permeant change that I could count on going forward. But it never was. And so, shortly after buying my stallion, I slipped backwards again. Not very far. I could still ride Lady for short periods and breed a mare or two. But I couldn't ride my stallion very often and the breeding took a lot out of me. And again, I was back to the long, arduous process of getting well. Again, I was fighting not to push myself, trying to rest when I needed rest.

Now, as my writing lays it out before me, I see it: the pattern of my life. And perhaps it isn't just the winters that cause this cycle, cause this constant up and down. Perhaps it is the nature of this illness. Or maybe it is me. Maybe it is my constant overreaching that forces this cycle on me. If that is the case, then there is hope. If I can change at last, stop overreaching for real and for always, then my life could be stable for once. Can I do that? Is it possible when I feel the joy of life flooding me again, not to leap into it with both feet and do, do, *do*?

As I sort this out Dave and I have realized that we can't run this ranch alone. Even with minimal animals. Even if it's just us and the land. There is wood to bring in and buildings to repair and fences to mend. So, we made some additions to the ranch besides animals. We found a few like-minded people who love this life and want to live up here; my cousin, Ben, his girlfriend, and a man they met through work. We gave them a place to live in exchange for help around the ranch and that made a difference. I have in mind that eventually the ranch would become a community of people all working together to make our way in the world. I suppose in its own small way it already is.

So here I am, trying to build up my strength as best I know how. I am once again surrounded by animals, even if not so many as there once was. I am even making some money by breeding my stallion to outside mares. I only take on a few each year, not wanting to push myself beyond my limits again. Dave is finally getting to stand down a little, thank goodness, and catch his breath. I don't know how we will manage the financial mess, but I try to trust that somehow that will work itself out. I get worn out easily and sleep most afternoons. A few times a week I sleep until noon, then go back to bed by one and sleep until dinner. Often, I spend days on the couch, not up for much else. I settle in my favorite spot with an afghan across my lap. My big orange cat comes and lays himself across my belly, just missing being sprawled across my keyboard as I type. I reach around him, my hands poised over the keys at an awkward angle. My little gray cat curls up beside my hip, purring loudly. My cousin's little dog settles on my legs, both propped up by the footrest of my recliner. His head hangs down off the footrest into thin air and he snores softly. Kaladin curls up just under my legs, as close to me as he can get without being on the couch. I watch out the big picture window as the golden fall sun beats down on our still-green yard and the horses graze in the pasture. Dave works upstairs in his home office, Ben around the ranch and his girlfriend and our friend in town. And I rest. In between resting I do what I can, but always, always I rest.

***

The summer of 2019, the year of the Covid pandemic, was one of the most social years of my life. I was surrounded by people I loved. By the end of that summer, I would spend my days riding my horse and having long talks with friends and in the evenings, gathering around a table for dinner with my cousin and my husband and everyone who lived at the ranch. This was the height of the Covid epidemic and while the rest of the world was isolated, the ranch was an active, social world. Oh, we were isolating. But we were isolating together.

***

I had continued to recover until I could ride for an hour at a time a couple times per week, as long as that was all I did, and I spent most of the remaining time resting. In January of 2019, I watched the coverage of Covid-19 and wondered what the big deal was. By March I knew. As I listened to the mounting death toll and the long list of symptoms, I was very clear: I didn't think I would survive that.

As the world shut down, we called a family council. I was just coming out of my big crash, just starting to be able to sit up long enough to share dinner with my family or work on my computer. Dave and I sat down with my cousin Ben and his girlfriend. The two of them had moved out here a few years before and traded out rent for work around the ranch. They lived in an apartment above our garage and the four of us made up the permanent "family" presently living on the ranch. During the summer, my mother lived in the log cabin we had built for her across one of the pastures from the house. My nieces had taken to spending most of the summer with us and friends and family came out regularly to visit. It wasn't unusual, during the summer months, to have 13 people here at a time, sleeping in all available corners and gathering around the table at dinner.

I had learned long ago that if I were to have guests around, I had to do the hosting thing differently than most people. I couldn't take care of all these people or keep up with the housework or the cooking for so many. Every Sunday we sat down and mapped out who would be here, assigning everyone nights to cook and nights to clean up and setting a day every week when everyone pitched in to vacuum and dust and basically clean the house. We assigned guests daily jobs such as gathering eggs, feeding the chickens, and watering the gardens. We called those meetings, "Family Council," and used them to divide up any jobs that needed doing. We also used those meetings to discuss any problems or issues that had come up around the ranch that week.

So, we called a family council to talk about Covid. Everyone agreed that I was at high risk and needed to be protected from exposure at all costs. Ultimately, we decided that Ben and Meghan would quit their jobs and we would provide them with food as well as rent so they could work exclusively at the ranch, for us. Both were new enough to the area that they weren't established in long term careers, and both were young enough that they could live simply for a time with little income. Dave's company had just instituted a work from home rule, so the four of us hunkered down and set about isolating ourselves at the ranch.

We rarely left the ranch for the rest of that year. One person would go into town each month for groceries. We would put an order in online and do contactless pick up. When the designated town person got home, they stripped off all their clothes, put them in the washer and immediately showered before interacting with anyone else. Then Dave, Ben, and Meghan would wipe down all the groceries with Lysol just to be safe.

I had just begun to recover enough to reach the boredom stage when Covid hit. I was bored with sitting in the house all the time but not really up for doing anything else yet. Everyone else had been busy with their lives, going off to work every day, and I had been getting more and more lonely. Then Covid—and everyone stayed home.

I loved it. Not the people-are-dying-and-the-world-is-crashing-down-around-us part, but the part where I suddenly had company, and everyone was around all the time. I hadn't had this much social interaction in years.

Come summer my family decided that the best place for my mother (also high risk) and the kids (who had been stuck in their rooms doing online school alone for months) was at the ranch. My brother drove everyone out here, driving straight through the night and taking along a camping toilet so they didn't have to use public restrooms. We had shut down our normal parade of guests so the 9 of us sequestered at the ranch together, riding horses (when I was up for it) and bottle-feeding baby goats. I was surrounded by people and activity. I had all the help I needed with the work of life and my recovery. Even after the summer ended, one of the kids stayed on, attending on-line school from the ranch for another few months. She did her zoom meetings, kept up with her classwork, and spent the rest of the day helping move hay, feed animals or clean barns. Her parents, who still needed to go to work, had decided that this was a better choice than her being sequestered in her suburban house, alone all day.

And so, I spent one of the more active, social years of my life riding out the Covid epidemic at the ranch. I was doing so well, in fact, that we decided that winter to send me south in the hopes that my recovery could continue and not do its usual stalling out during wintertime. We found a remote cabin in the middle of the Arizona desert and rented it for two months. Ben drove me out there, minimizing stopping and steeped in masks and hand sanitizer. He stayed for two weeks to enjoy the desert and get me set up with everything I would need for the next two months. Then he took the car and drove home, leaving me with two months' worth of food and no way to leave my cabin. I saw no other human being until the end of my stay, when Dave came down to get me, spending the last two weeks in the desert with me.

My little cabin was quite a find—it looked like a moon base, all covered in metal siding and sitting in the middle of the Painted Desert. It had good Wi-Fi and minimal electricity and bordered the Petrified Forest National Park. I walked in the desert every day and made myself meals of canned beans and diced tomatoes. My phone worked most of the time and I spent my days writing this book. As I sat there writing among the tumbleweed and sagebrush, I realized that my mind, which had shut down with my illness to the point that I often struggled just to form sentences, was working again. I reveled in my working brain.

When I returned to the ranch in the spring, Covid restrictions were easing, and my cousin's girlfriend went back to work. I tried to be happy for her but in fact I had liked it a lot more when she was around most of the time. Ben kept working at the ranch full time, but he was busy with ranch work, so as things went back to normal, I found myself once again getting lonely. But then the kids and my mom came out for the summer and this time, with all of us vaccinated, we were able to welcome friends and family to the ranch again. So, we started a busy summer and I prepared to start a Master's Degree program in Creative Writing, one of my solutions to the need to take it easy physically while my mind awoke. Life slowly crept back to normal for a while. But only for a while. By fall, Covid numbers were on the rise again and as I began my first semester of on-line school, we began talking about limiting my exposure and wearing masks once more. And so it goes, in this post-Covid world, the ups and downs, the starts and stops. But with vaccinations available and drastically reducing the amount of damage Covid usually did, we were no longer afraid for my life.

CHAPTER 24

Going to Mass With Dad

This week my family attended mass with my father for the last time.

Life-long Catholic, during the last decade of his life my dad went to mass every morning. He hadn't wanted us raised Catholic. He had too many issues with the politics of the Catholic Church. This wasn't the life he wanted for his kids, so he went every Sunday of my childhood to my mother's church where we attended as a family. Yet it was the Catholic Church which spoke the language of his heart. As I got older, I would sometimes make an effort to go to mass with him when I visited. I would sit in church, unmoved by the ritual and formality of the Catholic mass, and pray my own prayers, separate from what was going on around me. Afterward, he would introduce me, always proud, to those he knew. I think it meant a lot to him to have me there. So, I went.

My father spent his life seeking to be more like God, and I must say I know few who have embodied the pure acceptance and enjoyment of others, the spirit of service and the will to love as deeply as he has.

As he got older, my dad moved into a beautiful little retirement village, side by side with my stepmother, his wife. They had a busy social life with the other people at the center.

But then age started to take its toll. Dad was no longer able to follow complex discussions of ideas and philosophy. For a man with a PhD and four master's degrees, this was a major change. He forgot basic words. Who are you, what value do you hold, when your mind is no longer your own? But even in this, his loss, he left a gift for me. Because watching him I answered that question.

My father is not the books or the ideas or the discussions he loved so much. Those are wonderful things about him. But they are like a sweater he puts on—not part of him at his core. His trust in God and love of others defines who he truly is. At his core, my father is a gentle, calm presence. At his core, he is love, a quiet love. My mother loves by throwing out her arms and spinning in circles, laughing, and singing as loud as she can. My father's love is very different. He loves inside himself like strength permeating everything around him. He keeps his love so close, that some may not even know it's there, but it creates a foundation around him as solid as a rock, which you can feel if you pay attention.

***

Three days before his 90th birthday, my dad had a stroke. His right side went numb, and he fell. When his wife came back from coffee hour to see why he had not met her there as planned, she found him on the kitchen floor.

Though his right side was paralyzed, and his words were slurred, a quick response by paramedics and hospital workers stopped and quickly began to reverse the damage. That night he called me laughing and talking, his ironic sense of humor spilling out over the whole conversation. I wanted to rush to him like he once did to me and sit in his hospital room, feeling out of place and useless, but being there all the same. But Covid had put restrictions on hospital visits, and he wasn't allowed any visitors besides his wife. So, I sat at home and thought of him, called him on the phone once a day and waited. He was doing well. They expected a full recovery. He had a couple of weeks of physical therapy in front of him but all in all we got lucky.

We knew we wouldn't always be lucky in this way. He was 90, after all, and someday time would claim its due. Until then I would go to him when I could and sit with him, talking about life or my day or nothing at all. And it wouldn't matter if he forgot things sometimes, couldn't find his words, or repeated a story he just told me. It wouldn't matter if there were moments when he thought I was my sister or forgot what year it was. Because those are not important things. What is important is that I was there, as much as I could be, with this man who had shaped my life, who held me in the crook of his arm when I was born and, on whose feet, I stood to learn to dance. This man who walked me endlessly up and down the hallway when I couldn't sleep, bouncing me up and down, singing, "Hiking to the Yukon," who told me pollywog stories and took me square dancing, just the two of us, for years. What is important is that I was there, soaking up every moment I could get with this man, this blessed man who has created the foundation upon which I stand, who has taught me, not though words but through actions, what God is.

And when I visit, I try to go to mass with my dad. Last Monday I went again. This time dressed in black and with my whole family beside me. This time I didn't sit beside my father. He lay in a box near the front of the church while we sat in the pews. The priests recited the rituals. The deacons sang a prayer. It was not the kind of service we would have chosen for ourselves. The prayers were not our own, there was very little personal about it. They didn't let us speak about him or share our own thoughts. It wasn't the kind of goodbye that we usually experience at funerals in our mother's tradition. But that's okay.

We said goodbye the night before at the visitation when dozens of people filled the hall, telling stories about him and sharing their love for him. We said goodbye after the service when the family took up two large tables at a local restaurant and talked and laughed and told stories about his life. The Catholic service, wasn't my goodbye. It wasn't comforting in the way funerals usually are for me. Instead, it was a chance, one last chance, to honor my father and this path that he loved, to stand beside him and pay tribute to something which was sacred to him. It was my chance to attend mass with my father, one last time.

CHAPTER 25

Almost Fifty

As I write this book, I am almost fifty. I'm not sure how that happened, though looking back, I have enough stories to fill twice that many years. Still, I don't feel fifty. But then, who does?

I live on my ranch in Montana, breeding horses and raising orphaned kittens and sitting in my hammock chair on my deck with friends. I'm still filled with wonder at the birth of a new foal, and I still cry if an orphaned kitten doesn't survive. I still struggle with raising our own meat and I still take on baby sheep and goats, dress them in onesies and raise them in the house. I am still grateful for Dave and my family and all those who helped me to hold on to this life through it all.

I've learned a bit, too. I try not to take on quite so much at once. I am clearer now about the price I pay when I push this body too hard. I've learned to leave Montana in the winters whenever possible. More often than not, when I go into the wilderness for days, I take a friend with me. I leave riding wild horses to younger folk and spend my days on the back of my old, reliable mare who reads my mind like an open book and can sense my needs like Kaladin does.

There are days when I curse this illness and this body and resent that there are so many things I cannot do. But those days are increasingly fewer and farther between. The truth is, I love my life, and I am grateful for every difficult, struggle-filled minute of it. I still hope someday to shed this illness and ride my horse the entire length of the Pacific Crest Trail or take in a foster child or two. But if there is one thing I've learned, it's that those dreams are not the measure of my life. The measure of my life is not what I may or may not do tomorrow. The measure of my life is what I do today.

Today I turn the soil in my garden and draw diagrams of the planting to come. I race my mare up grass covered hills and wander with her through deep forests with tall trees. I sit in hammocks and read books that I love. I throw balls for my dog and try to convince Dave that we should take on just one more baby lamb to raise in the house just one more time. I travel to Arizona to the winters. And I plan for summer when my nieces will fill my house to bursting with laughter and chaos.

These are the things that are the measure of my life now. These glorious, beautiful things. I have plenty of dreams for tomorrow. But they are no longer the yardstick I use to determine my happiness. They will be if they will be or something else will be instead. As long as today is where my focus is, I cannot say that I truly lack for anything. Because today I have a glorious life.

Acknowledgement

I Want to thank my mom, who was my primary editor, and my niece, Jessica, who also did a lot of editing for this project. I also want to thank my publicist, Jess Wilder, who went above and beyond to make this book a success and my publisher, Krish Singh, who puts great time and effort into publishing first time authors, a group many publishers won't take risks on.

Milton Keynes UK
Ingram Content Group UK Ltd.
UKHW030748221024
449869UK00004B/262